THE ARCHITECTURE OF DIPLOMACY

The British Ambassador's Residence in Washington

THE ARCHITECTURE OF DIPLOMACY

The British Ambassador's Residence in Washington

Anthony Seldon
and **Daniel Collings**

Foreword by **HRH The Prince of Wales**

Photography by Eric Sander
Orchid photography by James Osen

Flammarion

CONTENTS

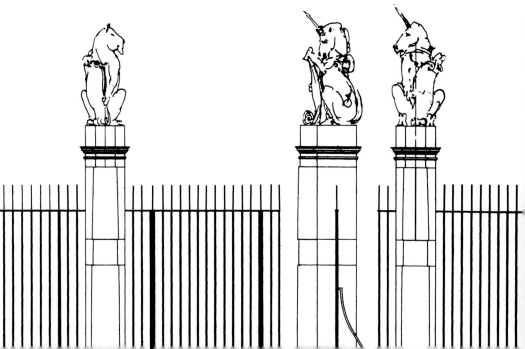

For over eighty years, the British Ambassador's Residence in Washington has stood as a magnificent symbol and a practical manifestation of the special relationship between the United States and the United Kingdom.

Commissioned in the aftermath of the First World War, a conflict which brought Britain and America closer than ever, it was completed in 1930 as an appropriately bold statement of the importance of the links between the peoples and governments of the two countries.

It is the only North American example of the work of Sir Edwin Landseer Lutyens, one of Britain's greatest architects of the early twentieth century and the master planner of the city of New Delhi. Lutyens designed the Residence when he was at the height of his powers, fresh from completing the iconic Cenotaph in central London. It was conceived, in the words of the diplomat and politician Harold Nicolson, to be "English in character and to afford opportunities for lavish entertainment." The style, with its red brick exterior, pavilion rooves and high, ornamented chimneys, is that of a Queen Anne country house, with additional touches reminiscent of New England colonial and Virginia plantation architecture, in deference to the host nation. The gardens, as so often in the case of Lutyens' architectural masterpieces, are inspired by the designs of the great English gardener, Gertrude Jekyll.

Today, the house continues to bring Britons and Americans from all walks of life together to celebrate and strengthen the enduring bond of friendship. Indeed, it has been a particularly special pleasure to stay in the Residence and to experience its diplomatic impact on several occasions over many years, most recently at a reception for British and American military service charities in 2011. Despite the scale and grandeur of the Residence, I could not help but observe how it has managed to make successive Ambassadors, their families and the literally thousands of people who have visited or stayed there, feel at home.

This book tells the story and demonstrates the beauty of this remarkable house. It highlights the Residence's vital contribution to international diplomacy and celebrates the work of a remarkable architect. I can only hope that it will also encourage future generations to continue to treasure the cultural and diplomatic legacy of this unique building.

HRH The Prince of Wales

PREFACE

Edwin Lutyens has been one of the key spiritual influences of my life. As a child, I first saw his work at Lindisfarne on Holy Island in my native Northumberland. In London, now home to my wife Shellard and myself, his buildings are a constant stimulus and on Remembrance Sunday each November the nation honours our war dead around the Cenotaph he designed. The very essence of the English countryside is defined by his quintessential country houses. From the poignancy of his First World War cemeteries in Belgium and in France to the magnificence of Imperial Delhi his architecture and designs are ubiquitously inspirational.

It was fertile soil, therefore, into which the Westmacotts planted, one evening on the Terrace of the Residence, the idea of supporting the creation of this book. The 25th anniversary of the foundation of Campbell Lutyens in February 1988 was upon us. Richard Lutyens, my eponymous fellow founding partner, ho died in 1994 at the early age of 45, was a great nephew of Sir Edwin. What better way could there be to commemorate that anniversary than by helping to bring to a wider audience the glories of Edwin Lutyens' unique masterpiece in North America?

Our firm's daily task as corporate financiers is to enable investors worldwide to access long-term successful partnerships within the private equity and private infrastructure sectors. Edwin Lutyens built in partnership with his patrons for future generations. He laid his extraordinary creativity and originality on the foundations of a deep Classical sensibility. He was the master of the marriage of the local vernacular with wider architectural traditions. His work of all kinds had the perennial qualities of integrity, honesty and humour. We aspire at Campbell Lutyens to travel in his footsteps.

Shellard and our children – Milo, Coco and Rollo – join me in congratulating Sir Peter and his wife Susan Nemazee Westmacott for their initiative and lucubration in conceptualising and bringing this book to fruition. It is, I believe, a worthy companion to the magnificent book on the Residence in Paris which they created during Sir Peter's ambassadorship to France.

PAGE 2 Lutyens' stunning Main Corridor comprises the principal east-west axis of the Residence.
PAGES 4–5 Elevation of the Residence gate from Lutyens' original drawings.
PAGE 6 An exquisitely carved unicorn sits atop the gatepost overseeing visitors entering the driveway to the Residence.
FACING PAGE The west side of the Residence, viewed from the steps leading up to the swimming pool.

John Campbell
Chairman and Co-Founder
Campbell Lutyens and Co. Ltd

INTRODUCTION

When the British government decided, in the 1920s, that it was time to build an Embassy in Washington which reflected both the importance of our links to the United States and our sense of Britain's standing in the world, it was little surprise that it turned to the man who was our pre-eminent architect at the time, Sir Edwin Lutyens. It asked him to design a building which was to be both office suite and grand residence – and which turned out to be the only house he ever built in the Western Hemisphere.

More surprising is the fact that, despite the importance of the building, the events and the diplomatic history that it witnessed, no full history of the Embassy has been attempted before now. This volume, for which I am indebted to Anthony Seldon, Daniel Collings, our sponsor the Campbell family and our editor Suzanne Tise-Isoré, has been written to put that right. Both the concept and its realization owe a great deal to the tireless enthusiasm of my wife Susan Nemazee Westmacott.

So rapidly did our relations with the US expand during and on either side of the Second World War that by 1960 we had had to supplement Lutyens' masterpiece with a huge concrete office block next door. As a result, the building he left us is now known simply as the Residence, even if the part most easily visible from Massachusetts Avenue has become a mix of staff apartments and office accommodation for the British Council.

The Residence is the heart of Britain's diplomatic presence in what Americans know as the nation's capital. It receives around fifteen thousand guests a year, for an extraordinary variety of functions – two or three sometimes going on at the same time. They range from one-on-one meals through intimate breakfasts, lunches and dinners when political, business and military personalities come together to discuss what's happening in the world, to major dinners, receptions, barbeques, conferences and garden parties. Rarely does a senior visitor from London not stay in the house. The one constant theme is the depth, breadth, importance and regularity of the links between our two countries.

Many countries claim to have special, unique or historic relationships with others. Sometimes they do. But the reality of modern diplomacy is that nothing can be taken for granted. A special relationship is not conferred, like a title, but has to be earned, continuously. Promoting your country abroad requires an unrelenting effort to develop links, spread knowledge, and make an impact, making the best possible use of the resources at your disposal. The people who are best placed to make a difference to our interests are, increasingly, busy and in great demand. They will only come to an event at a foreign embassy if it is worthwhile, attended by others it's useful for them to see, and – with luck – enjoyable.

FACING PAGE Lutyens' grand Portico, which embraces Palladian neo-classicism, Colonial Williamsburg and possibly the White House. From the Terrace beneath, visitors walk down to the Lower Terrace, below which the lawn begins. A more elegant outside space in Washington would be hard to find.

That's the challenge facing an ambassador in the twenty-first century, who, in addition to making a personal impact, has to be on top of the issues of the day, able to interpret them to his or her capital, and actively negotiate in support of the national interest. Gone are the times when a head of government might observe, as President Thomas Jefferson once did to his secretary of state, that he hadn't heard from his ambassador in Spain for two years, and that, if he didn't hear from him for another one, it might be a good idea to write him a letter.

Doing the job is immeasurably easier if you have Lutyens on your side. The house which this book seeks to illustrate and explain has already seen – or contributed to – a huge number of events of importance to the links between our two countries: state banquets, Churchillian visits, critical negotiations – even, on my watch, the first meeting between the newly-elected President François Hollande of France and Prime Minister David Cameron as well as the last dinner Hillary Clinton attended as secretary of state.

I have always felt that the human dimension of architecture is important. Buildings are after all places where people live, work and come together. In our case, the effect is enhanced by the presence in the house of fine works of art provided by the UK Government Art Collection. As a result, 'The Architecture of Diplomacy' is a title perfectly suited to the story and images of how we have sought to promote the UK's interests in, and relations with, the United States over the last eighty years.

I know I am not the first of those lucky enough to live in this remarkable house to have been both humbled and excited by the challenge of living up to Lutyens' expectations as I entertain in the Ballroom under the watchful eye of Andy Warhol's Queen Elizabeth II; or to have sat in admiration of the symmetry and wood panelling of Lutyens' library as I plough through boxes of official papers at night, seeking inspiration. On one of his recent visits, former President Bill Clinton told me that if he had the good fortune to live in this house, he would never leave the library. I know what he meant.

I hope you will enjoy discovering in the following pages why this Residence, its architecture and its garden have such a special place in the diplomatic history of the United Kingdom in the United States.

Sir Peter Westmacott
British Ambassador to the United States of America

FACING PAGE The Residence viewed through the trees of the surrounding garden, which is such an integral part of the Embassy.

THE RESIDENCE HOSTS A VARIETY OF EVENTS TO PROMOTE
BILATERAL RELATIONS AND THE BEST OF BRITAIN, FROM BUSINESS
TO EDUCATION, ART, TRADE, FILM AND SPORT.

On these pages is a collage of photographs of events held at the Residence and of personalities visiting the house, including The Queen, The Prince of Wales and The Duchess of Cornwall, Prince Harry, Prime Minister David Cameron, Foreign Secretary William Hague, Chancellor of the Exchequer George Osborne, Vice President Joe Biden, Associate Justice Stephen Breyer, Secretaries of State Henry Kissinger, Hillary Clinton and John Kerry, Secretary of the Treasury Timothy Geithner, IMF Managing Director Christine Lagarde, Senator John McCain, sculptor Antony Gormley, entrepreneur Sir Richard Branson and the cast of Downton Abbey.

'The Finest Embassy in the World' The Washington Post, 1929

THE BRITISH EMBASSY IN WASHINGTON, WHICH OPENED in 1930 while Herbert Hoover was President of the United States, was designed by Sir Edwin Lutyens (1869–1944), the pre-eminent British architect of his day. A blend of the English country house tradition with the American Colonial style, it is the only building Lutyens designed in the United States. For more than eighty years, the British Embassy in Washington has been regarded as the premier diplomatic address in the city, and its most gracious and aesthetically pleasing. As *The Washington Post* proclaimed shortly before it opened, it would prove 'the finest in the world'.[1]

Lutyens was at the height of his career when, in 1925, he was approached by the British government to design the new embassy in Washington. He had first come to prominence in the 1890s as an architect of elegant and spacious country houses in Britain, articulating a vernacular English style. In the 1900s, he began to combine this approach with Classical traditions. His fame grew significantly when the British government commissioned him to help create a new capital in India, then ruled by the British, at New Delhi, to replace Calcutta as the seat of government. The pinnacle of his career was the building of the Viceroy's House (1912–31) at the heart of the new city, which became the official residence of the president after India received its independence in 1947. The First World War (1914–18) brought Lutyens' still further to international prominence. As a principal architect of Britain's Imperial War Graves Commission, Lutyens influenced the design of hundreds of war cemeteries and memorials, as well as designing the largest monument of the war, the 'Memorial to the Missing of the Somme' (1927–32), in France. Better known still is his iconic Cenotaph (unveiled 1920) in central London, a won-derfully simple monument that has become the national focus for mourning Britain's war dead in all wars ever since.

Diplomatic relations between Britain and the United States were first established in 1785, just two years after the end of the Revolutionary War. Britain's first diplomats were itinerant, and Britain acquired a permanent building (known as a 'legation') only in 1876, on Connecticut Avenue within half a mile of the White House. Constructed in the decade following the American Civil War, this reflected the growing value being attached to the Anglo-American relationship on both sides of the Atlantic. The workload grew considerably, and by 1900 the Embassy was considered too small, while the noise of trams running on the street and rattling the windows added to demands for a bigger and more secluded residence. Discussions were put on hold with the outbreak of war in Europe, and it was not until 1925 that the government finally took the decision to go ahead.

A rural site was chosen on Massachusetts Avenue, further away from the White House and Capitol Hill, in an area overgrown by brush. It was an odd plot to have chosen. The land rose not only upwards with Massachusetts Avenue, but also sloped away from the road, giving Lutyens the problem of erecting his structure on ground which angled in two directions. The plot was also awkwardly shaped and remarkably confined, in the shape of an inverted P, with the base of the capital letter adjoining the road, and the wider area away from it. Many would have been overwhelmed by the problems the site presented. A distinguishing characteristic of great architects is that they turn such difficulties to their advantage, and that is exactly what Lutyens did here.

Construction took place between January 1928 and 1930. To the difficulties of terrain were added the problems of finding the money for Lutyens' grand design (he was renowned for being an expensive architect). The Wall Street Crash of October 1929 hampered construction, as did opposition from trade unions. Lutyens' other projects, above all New Delhi, were further distractions, requiring long winter visits to oversee the work. Constant battles over finance with the Treasury in London, and disagreements over the designs with the British ambassador in Washington, ground Lutyens down, but he stuck to the task relentlessly until the building was opened in May 1930.

PAGES 16–17 The full façade of the Residence. Lutyens designed it to face southwards towards the garden rather than eastwards towards the street. It is thus hidden from passers-by and even from visitors to the building if they do not step outside into the garden.

FACING PAGE A gate that leads from the driveway up to the back of the house. This geometrical design, in cypress wood, and the steps beyond are typical Lutyens' features.

The Embassy from the air, taken in 1939. The densely packed trees growing behind give a sense of how wild and remote this part of Washington remained at this stage. This additional land was later purchased for the Embassy and the trees were removed, in part to make way for a new Chancery building. Also visible is how Lutyens has laid out the gardens, in a complex series of terraces, stairs and walkways, applying his same skills and love of geometry to the architecture of the gardens as he does to the building adjacent to it.

The Embassy is composed of two distinct sections: the Chancery, designed as office space for the diplomatic staff, and the Residence, where the ambassador was to live. Although a new functional office building was erected on an adjacent site between 1957 and 1960, the Residence has remained the unbroken home of the British ambassador since 1930. Lutyens was responsible too for designing the elegant gardens, which are such an integral feature of his overall concept. Inspired by his long working relationship with the distinguished garden designer Gertrude Jekyll (1843–1932), Lutyens conceived the perfect English garden and transplanted it to Washington. Countless garden parties have been hosted at the Embassy, the largest for over five thousand guests, who find themselves transported back to the old world as they wander along the garden's many paths flanked by flowerbeds.

The Embassy has been at the very heart of Anglo-American relations since 1930. When Lutyens was first asked to design the building, relations were at a low ebb: confidential papers reveal there was even talk of a possible war between the United States and Britain. The election of Franklin D. Roosevelt in November 1932 contributed to a slow process of rapprochement, which intensified after Winston Churchill became prime minister in May 1940 and the entry of the United States into the Second World War in December 1941. In the post-war years, relations were close throughout much of the Cold War period, peaking in the early 1960s during the presidency of John F. Kennedy, and in the 1980s when Ronald Reagan was president and Margaret Thatcher prime minister.

The Embassy has played host to a never-ending stream of visitors, including most presidents since Hoover. Many members of the royal family have visited since King George VI made his famous visit in 1939, in the months leading up to the Second World War, becoming the first British head of state ever to come to the United States. Winston Churchill was a regular and delighted visitor, as was Margaret Thatcher. During President Kennedy's time in the White House, from 1961 to 1963, the Embassy assumed particular importance. The ambassador, Sir David Ormsby Gore, was a close personal friend of the president and the Residence became witness to 'book club' meetings attended by Kennedy family notables and dinner dances lasting into the early hours of the morning.

Lutyens designed the supreme diplomatic Residence, outclassing not only its competitors in Washington, but countless others across the world. Unlike other elegant diplomatic houses, such as the British residences in Paris and Moscow, this was purpose-built. Its artistic success lies in the fusion of English and Classical architecture he knew so well, with Colonial American architecture seen at Williamsburg and Monticello. Its practical success lies in his genius in conceiving the space that would best serve successive ambassadors' needs. It is the work of a supreme master at the height of his powers, as successful, if not more so, than his work in New Delhi. The building stands today as proudly an emblem of Anglo-American cultural and diplomatic cooperation as it was when it first opened its doors in 1930.

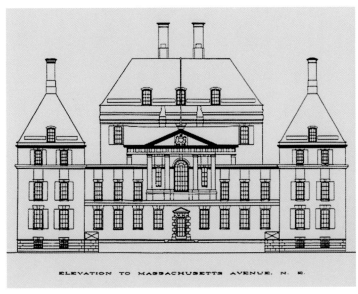

ELEVATION TO MASSACHUSETTS AVENUE. N. E.

FACING PAGE A contemporary view of Lutyens' Embassy from Massachusetts Avenue. At the front stands the Chancery, with the roof of the Residence clearly visible behind.
ABOVE Lutyens' original sketch of the entrance façade for the Embassy as seen from Massachusetts Avenue. Retained by Lutyens in his office, this sketch and many others are now kept by the Royal Institute of British Architects.
RIGHT Sir Edwin Landseer Lutyens, the architect of his generation, in 1924.

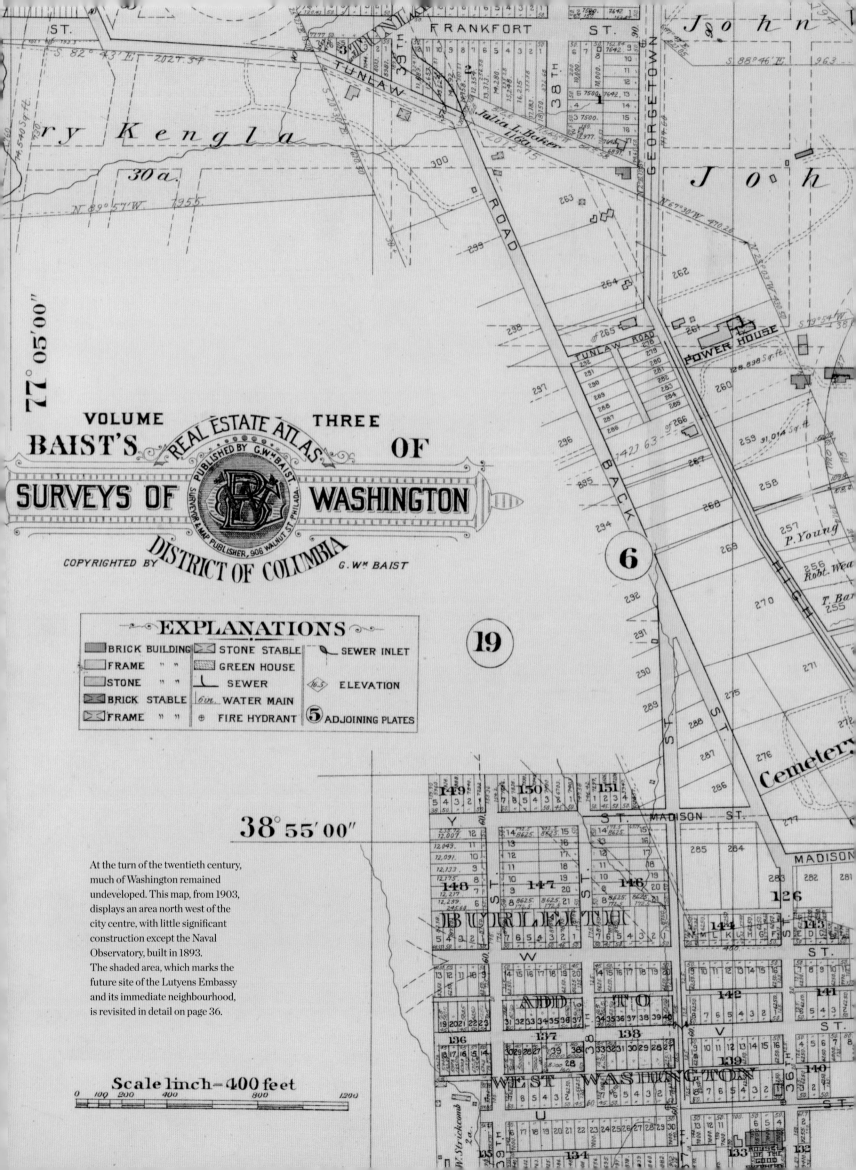

77° 05' 00"

VOLUME THREE
BAIST'S REAL ESTATE ATLAS OF
SURVEYS OF WASHINGTON
PUBLISHED BY G. Wm. BAIST.
SURVEYOR & MAP PUBLISHER, 906 WALNUT ST. PHILADA.
DISTRICT OF COLUMBIA
COPYRIGHTED BY G. Wm. BAIST

EXPLANATIONS

BRICK BUILDING	STONE STABLE	SEWER INLET
FRAME " "	GREEN HOUSE	
STONE " "	SEWER	ELEVATION
BRICK STABLE	6 in. WATER MAIN	
FRAME " "	FIRE HYDRANT	5 ADJOINING PLATES

38° 55' 00"

At the turn of the twentieth century,
much of Washington remained
undeveloped. This map, from 1903,
displays an area north west of the
city centre, with little significant
construction except the Naval
Observatory, built in 1893.
The shaded area, which marks the
future site of the Lutyens Embassy
and its immediate neighbourhood,
is revisited in detail on page 36.

Scale 1 inch = 400 feet

0   100 200   400   800   1200

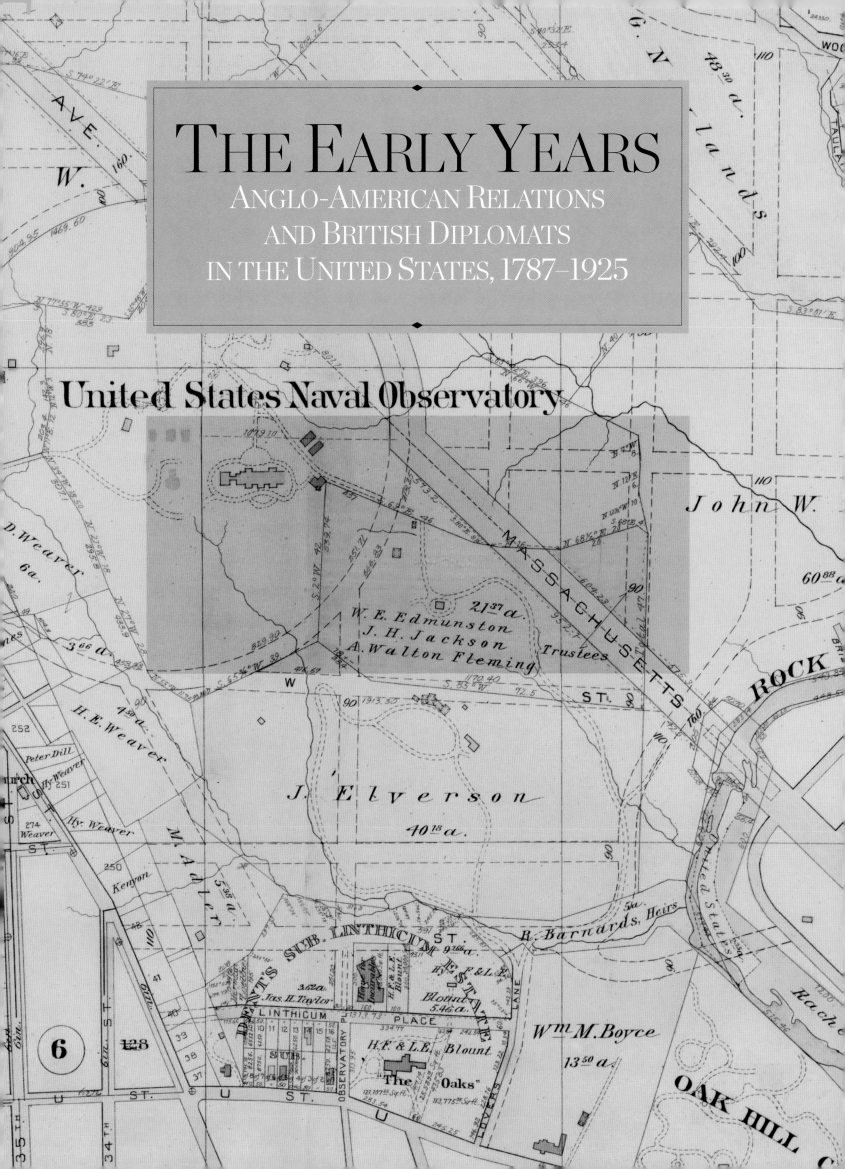

The Early Years

Anglo-American Relations
and British Diplomats
in the United States, 1787–1925

Henry Laurens (1724–1792) President of Congress (1777–1778) Painted 1791 1832-20

John Jay (1745–1829) Chief Justice of the United States Painted 1793 1832-21

John Adams (1735–1826) President of the United States. Painted 1792 1832-22

George Hammond (1763–1853) First British Minister to the United States. Painted 1792 1832-23

William Temple Franklin (c.1760–1823) Grandson of Benjamin Franklin. Painted 1790 1832-24

AUTHORS' NOTE

From Minister to Ambassador

In the late eighteenth century, the new American republic was a decidedly minor player on the world stage. In those days, nations reserved the title of 'ambassador' for diplomats sent to major powers. Therefore Britain's representation in the United States consisted of a 'minister', a diplomatic envoy one rank below that of 'ambassador'. This minister (formally, from 1796, the 'envoy extraordinary and minister plenipotentiary') oversaw a 'legation', rather than an 'embassy'. Only in 1893, as the United States emerged to become a major nation, was British representation upgraded. Sir Julian Pauncefote then became Britain's first 'ambassador' to the United States overseeing what was then officially a British Embassy.

Embassies, Residences and Chanceries

The terminology used to describe the buildings housing Britain's representatives in the United States has evolved considerably over the years. From 1893, Pauncefote lived and worked, with his staff, in an 'Embassy' on Connecticut Avenue. In the late 1920s, Lutyens was commissioned to design a 'Residence', in which the ambassador and his family would live and entertain, and a 'Chancery', to house the diplomatic staff. Collectively these two buildings were known as the 'Embassy'. By the late 1950s, this Embassy became far too small for a greatly expanded diplomatic staff and so a new building was constructed directly adjacent and to the north of the Lutyens site. Known initially as the 'New Chancery', this building became the working hub for Britain's diplomats in Washington. Today it is often referred to as the 'Embassy', distinguishing it from the 'Residence', which remains the home of the ambassador, and the 'Old Chancery', which has taken on a variety of functions ranging from staff accommodation to offices for the British Council.

ABOVE The inclusion of George Hammond, Britain's first minister to the United States, in this collection of late eighteenth-century American notables helps demonstrate the enduring importance of Britain to the United States in the early years of the American Republic.

Early Years
Britain, America and Diplomatic Representation, 1776–1925

Independence, 1776–1810

No country likes to lose a large part of its possessions abroad against its will. If the country was Great Britain, the most powerful on earth, and the land it was to lose consisted of thirteen prosperous and fertile Colonies of two-and-a-half million people in the New World, the loss was all the greater to bear. British pride thus took a severe dent when, following the American Colonies' Declaration of Independence in 1776 and after seven years of bloody fighting, London was forced to yield sovereignty to the upstart former colonists. But a relationship born in anger and bloodshed was to become central to the foreign policies of both countries, from the Treaty of Paris in 1783, which terminated the Revolutionary War, until the present day.

The first US envoy to Britain was John Adams, one of the architects of American independence. So it was with some anxiety on both sides that he arrived at St James's Palace in London in June 1785 for an audience with the British monarch who had presided over the loss of the Colonies, King George III. Adams told the King that he wished to restore, 'the old good nature and the old good humour between people who, though separated by an ocean and under different governments, have the same language, a similar religion, and kindred blood'. It was to prove one of the most extraordinary meetings in the long history of Anglo-American relations. 'I was the last to consent to separation', the King told an apprehensive Adams. But in a spirit of magnanimity, he then announced, 'I have always said, as I say now, that I would be the first to meet the friendship of the United States as an independent power'.[1] As sign of new found stability, Britain sent its first envoy, George Hammond, to the United States in 1791.

Hammond, officially the first British resident minister, based himself in Philadelphia, the new country's temporary capital while Washington was being built, and its biggest port and city.

A middle-ranking diplomat, he was taking up a post few in London actively sought, but he made a success of it, overseeing the establishment of formal relations between Britain and America. Anthony Merry became the first British minister to be based in Washington itself, in 1803, but in those days there was no settled diplomatic residence. Diplomats instead rented accommodation, and the next ten ministers moved houses frequently.

The relationship between Britain and America now went through a series of distinct phases. Only gradually, as the relationship assumed more significance, did Britain's diplomatic representation in the United States grow in both size and importance – not until the 1870s was a permanent building established.

Uncertainty and a mutual wariness characterised the first phase of Anglo-American relations, from 1783 to 1810. Economically the thirteen states that made up the new United States were still dependent on Great Britain, while British forts remained on territory in the Old Northwest, theoretically ceded to the United States. Yet not everyone in the new republic was content with this relationship, preferring instead to boost ties to Britain's great rival, France, which had supported the Colonies during the Revolutionary War.

Much of the eighteenth century had seen intense rivalry between Britain and France. Following the French Revolution, from 1789, French military adventurism culminated in the Napoleonic Wars of the early 1800s. With France at war against Britain, opinion in the United States was polarised. Key figures such as George Washington, the first president, and John Adams, who succeeded him in 1797, supported the British, while others, including Thomas Jefferson, who became the third president in 1801, backed the French. Jefferson, the author of the Declaration of Independence in 1776, went on to double the size of the country as president with the purchase of the Louisiana Territory from France in 1803.

War and Peace, 1810–65

Relations between Britain and the United States rapidly deteriorated into the 'War of 1812'. The conflict originated in disagreements over trade emanating from Britain's long war with Napoleonic France, British support of Native American tribes resisting US territorial expansion, and British anxieties about the annexation of Canada by the United States. The Americans were particularly disturbed by the British policy of impressment, whereby the Royal Navy would seize American sailors and force them to serve on British ships.

Fought on land and sea, the war lasted nearly three years. In August 1814, British soldiers occupied Washington, the new US capital. The Americans received so little warning that the first lady, Dolley Madison, expecting her husband for dinner, had to flee the White House with moments to spare. The British burned the White House and every other public building in Washington with the exception of the Patent Office. That September the British attacked Baltimore, unleashing a vicious overnight bombardment from the sea on its defenders at Fort McHenry. The attack proved unsuccessful. Francis Scott Key, a lawyer seeking to negotiate the release of American prisoners, witnessed this from a British battleship where he was being held. The morning after the shelling, observing a large American flag rising from the Fort, Key was inspired to write the 'Star Spangled Banner', later adopted as the American national anthem.

For the United States then, these were formative years and this conflict was of seminal importance: some American historians view it as the Second War of Independence. But to Britain, it was always something of a sideshow. Having secured sufficient guarantees over maritime rights, and heavily distracted by the Duke of Wellington's military campaigns against France, London assented to peace in late 1814. For the United States, it was a major victory, ending once and for all British support for Native Americans, pushing the British out of key defensive positions in Ohio and beyond, and imparting great confidence to the still young United States.

With peace from 1815 came forty years of relative tranquillity as diplomatic relations matured. While America remained a nation of little international significance, the British Empire entered its golden age. Following the defeat of Napoleon at Waterloo in 1815, Britain had no serious global rival and the empire flourished, spreading throughout Asia and in Africa. This was the era, the so-called *Pax Britannia*, in which the Royal Navy really did rule the waves. The Industrial Revolution, which began in England in the later eighteenth century, had boosted British trade and fortunes. As knowledge spread across the Atlantic, America too benefited. The United States was still tightly tied to Britain economically, thus a steady flow of British credit proved crucial for the development of American canals, railways and factories. When political difficulties arose, as over the borders of British Columbia and the state of Washington, compromises were successfully negotiated.

The victory of Abraham Lincoln in the 1860 presidential election exacerbated simmering hostilities within the United States and triggered the secession of eleven slave states. During the Civil War that followed, Anglo-American tensions reached new heights. The northern states were constantly fearful that the British would side with the Confederacy, while in the seceded South there was disappointment at the lack of British support. The minister in Washington, Lord Lyons, had his work cut out reassuring both sides, though it is clear from contemporary documents that there was never any serious prospect that Britain would fight on the side of the Confederacy, much though some in the British Cabinet might have liked to have done so.

LEFT Expecting a victory over the British during the War of 1812, President James Madison ordered a feast prepared at the White House. When, instead, British forces defeated the Americans and took Washington, they helped themselves to Madison's largesse before setting fire to the White House, leaving the building a burnt-out shell (pen and ink drawing, late nineteenth century).

A New Harmony, 1865–1918

A new era of cordial relations, the closest so far, blossomed shortly after the end of the Civil War in 1865. The United States emerged from its post-war 'Reconstruction Era' a stronger and more confident nation, rapidly industrialising and spreading westwards, its expansion facilitated by new railways. The idea now took root of a common 'Anglo-Saxon heritage', a notion that suited the elites of both countries. Henry James helped build bridges between Britain and America, as did Charles Dickens, whose visit to the United States in 1867 on a reading tour was a wild success. More reliable and larger boats plied the Atlantic between Britain's ports and the United States, and cordiality between both countries was in the air. By the 1870s, Britain no longer viewed the United States as a dangerously radical country. Rather, it came to be admired as one which had successfully blended the extension of the electoral franchise with the interests of capital and the rights of property.

During the Civil War, the British legation, based in rented accommodation a block away from the White House, had become the largest and most important of the diplomatic missions in Washington. After the war, British diplomats worked assiduously to improve relations, supported by changing attitudes in London. Prime Minister William Gladstone's settlement of the *Alabama* Claims in 1872, brought by the US government against Britain for assistance to the Confederate cause during the Civil War, assuaged feelings previously much aggrieved. With a warming relationship – and more work than ever – pressure mounted for Britain's diplomats to work from a more permanent and professional residence in Washington.

The Washington of this period was a far cry from the city of today. With a population of around 130,000, much of the land outside a tiny centre remained undeveloped. Even at its heart, the city had only dirt roads and lacked sanitation. Washington may have been the nation's capital but it was also little more than a small town. Thus, when Britain became the first country to purchase land and construct a building for its diplomatic representatives, between 1873 and 1876, the choice of site aroused great interest. The address, at the corner of Connecticut Avenue and N Street, was only half a mile from the White House. Even so, this part of town was then considered a backwater and many wondered if anyone would ever visit. However, the new British legation proved popular with politicians and diplomats and, before the end of the century, the area around Connecticut Avenue had developed into Washington's main diplomatic hub.

In recognition of the increased importance of America in the world, and a new phase in relations with Britain, the 'legation' was officially upgraded to an 'embassy' in March 1893. Sir Julian Pauncefote (later Lord Pauncefote), minister in Washington since 1889, now became the first British ambassador to the United States. These were promising times for Anglo-American relations. When crises erupted they were settled peacefully. In 1895, when Britain threatened war against Venezuela over a boundary dispute, Washington insisted the claim be resolved by international arbitration. Pauncefote's personal legacy was to prove his successful negotiation with Secretary of State John Hay over America's role in Central America. Setting aside previous British efforts to check US influence, the Hay-Pauncefote Treaty of 1901 gave America the right to construct and control what became the Panama Canal. This was a crucial step as America spread its influence southwards. When Pauncefote died at the Embassy, in May 1902, he was held in such esteem that the flag at the White House was lowered to half-mast.

ABOVE Britain's first permanent Embassy building at 1300 Connecticut Avenue. Completed in 1876, it was a mark of pride for British diplomats, who became the first in Washington to acquire a permanent base. But by the early 1900s, it had fallen into disrepair and was simply too small to house Britain's expanded diplomatic presence. This painting by Arthur Franklin Musgrave dates from 1925 and today hangs in the upper floor of Lutyens' Residence.

LEFT Connecticut Avenue between 1882 and 1900, before the area became too commercialised and noisy for the work of Britain's diplomats.

FACING PAGE Lord Pauncefote (depicted between 1890 and 1902) was an accomplished diplomat and, for his age, a technological pioneer. The first diplomat to send a typewritten letter to the State Department, he inaugurated the era of typewritten communication among the diplomatic community.

author Harold Nicolson as still recapturing 'the charm of a pro-vincial, almost a county, capital', while the Embassy building 'with its balconies, its bow-windows and its sun blinds, produced the effect of a large villa at Newport'.[2] This idyllic image did not last long. In 1900, the increasing volume of work led to an extension to the Chancery, but within a few years even this proved inadequate. It was becoming clear that a totally new site was needed.

James Bryce, who had been a junior minister under Gladstone, was appointed British ambassador in early 1907. He quickly decided that the Embassy should now move further away from the city centre to provide more space. But he found little sympathy at the Office of Works in London, who claimed they did not have the money. Incensed, Bryce stressed that the existing building had become far too expensive to run and heat, the roof was leaking, and, to make matters worse, 'a double line of electric cars [trams] now runs in front of the house, and the noise is so great that when the windows of the front drawing room, and of the ambassador's sitting room are open those in these rooms can hardly hear them-selves speak'.[3] London, however, remained far from impressed by his case. Architects were sent to inspect the site and buildings, which they valued at £55,000, as against a likely cost of a new site and buildings at £90,000. The quest for a new Embassy faded and Bryce left in 1913, at the age of 74, a disappointed man.

His successor, Cecil Spring-Rice, a career diplomat, soon reached the same conclusion as his predecessor. The British Embassy, he wrote to the Office of Works, would 'shortly be the only private house in a street of shops and trams'. The area was now 'so noisy that ciphering and telephoning are a matter of great difficulty', while the work of the naval and military attachés upstairs was 'becoming impossible'.[4] Once again, such pleas fell on deaf ears. In April 1914, Sir Lionel Earle, the chief official at the Office of Works (who will assume great importance in the story to come) wrote to Spring-Rice: 'I am absolutely convinced that it would be impossible to get any money from the Treasury for building a new Embassy and for the purchase of [a new] site at this moment.'[5] In any case, storm clouds were beginning to gather over Europe and, within a few months, Britain was to be at war. All practical hopes of a new Embassy were shelved for the duration.

The First World War, 1914–18

The First World War changed the relationship between both countries fundamentally. Up to 1914, the United States was in-debted to Great Britain: from 1918 onwards, Britain was indebt-ed to the United States. As war swept across Europe from August 1914, President Woodrow Wilson declared American neutrality. The forces within the United States ranged against any involve-ment in the 'European War' were strong. No vital US interest was at stake and there was little prospect of any immediate gain to justify the risks.

The sinking of the British liner *Lusitania* by a German U-boat in May 1915 killed up to a hundred and thirty Americans. Despite strong protests from Washington, in February 1917 the Germans announced 'unrestricted' submarine warfare in the Atlantic, which meant that even US ships would be fair game. Later that month the Zimmermann telegram emerged, revealing German encourage-ment for Mexico to invade the United States, should Washington enter the conflict. That April, the United States joined the war against Germany. American munitions and food arrived in France and Belgium fairly quickly, but it was not until the summer of 1918 that American soldiers under General John Pershing arrived in great force, tipping the balance against the fading German power.

Tense Relations, 1918–30

After the war ended in November 1918, Wilson became the first American president to cross the Atlantic. He received a tumultuous welcome in Britain; his idealism caught the mood of the moment. But his message was not the 'brothers in arms' theme that many in the British establishment (and some back in America) had hoped for. At a state banquet at Buckingham Palace, dressed in a bland black suit in contrast to the bejewelled finery and uniforms around him, he declared: 'You must not speak of us who come over here as cousins, still less as brothers. We are neither. Neither must you think of us as Anglo-Saxons for that term can no longer be applied to the people of the United States.' What did hold both countries together, he said, was a

in the First World War. Greeted by enthusiastic crowds, Wilson himself was less enthusiastic about building closer ties with Britain.

FACING PAGE Sir Esme Howard, ambassador 1924–30, proved a great champion for constructing a new embassy in Washington. But his very firm views on what the building should accomplish later put him at odds with its architect.

PAGES 34–5 The *Porte-Cochère* with the Ambassador's Study above, the Chancery to the right and the Residence to the left. Ink, graphite and watercolour drawing by Cyril Farey, 1927.

'community of ideals and of interests'.[6] When those ideals and interests were intertwined, as they were during both World Wars and the Cold War, the relationship was immensely close. But, when they diverged, the relationship could become cold as ice.

After 1918, relations between both countries cooled markedly. Wilson dominated the Paris Peace Conference in 1919, and pressed hard for the establishment of the League of Nations. But the US Senate went on to reject both the Treaty of Versailles and US involvement in the League of Nations. A deep isolationism set in across America wedded to a belief that Britain had pushed the US into the First World War unnecessarily. Throughout the interwar years, Anglo-American relations were often tense. At the lowest point in 1928, the British official in charge of the American desk at the Foreign Office wrote a paper, circulated to the Cabinet: 'war is *not* unthinkable between the two countries', he insisted. 'On the contrary there are present all the factors which have made for war between States ... Great Britain is faced in the United States of America with a phenomenon for which there is no parallel in our modern history – a State twenty-five times as large, five times as wealthy, three times as populous, twice as ambitious.'[7]

It was a measure of America's growing strength and importance to Britain – not to mention the need to avoid a conflict – that

convinced London that it was time to upgrade Britain's diplomatic presence in Washington. Besides, the Embassy on Connecticut Avenue, now littered with temporary extensions following the upsurge in activity during the First World War, was simply no longer fit for purpose. Even the most budget-conscious officials in Whitehall could not deny that the building was now drastically too small and in poor repair. A move had become inevitable.

The new ambassador from 1924 was Esme Howard, a career diplomat who had previously represented Britain in Madrid. Before leaving for the United States, by boat, he went to a meeting in London with the Office of Works' Lionel Earle, who asked him to reflect on the wisdom of a move and report back. Within weeks of arrival in Washington, Howard wrote excitedly to say that he had held an interview with a 'Mr Wardman' 'one of the principal real estate leaders in Washington', who owns a piece of land 'on Massachusetts Avenue which I am going to look at next week'.[8] Howard took his private secretary, Henry Hopkinson, with him: 'surprisingly,' Hopkinson later wrote, 'the whole area was still covered with thick scrub and bushes. We found that the only way he and I could reach it comfortably was on horseback, pushing the branches out of our faces as we went up the narrow path'.[9] The rest, as they say, is history.

LUTYENS' MASTERPIECE

BUILDING A NEW EMBASSY
IN WASHINGTON, 1925–30

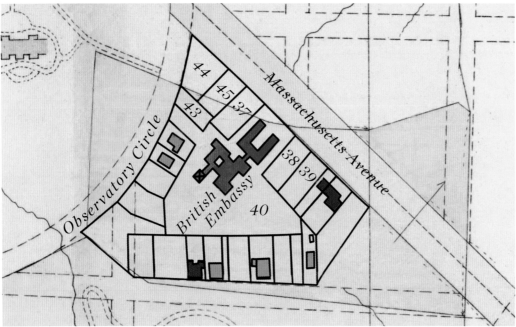

ABOVE The Chancery under construction, dating from approximately 1928. The outer driveway to the Residence had yet to be laid.

LEFT This map, reflecting developments by the early 1930s, shows the newly constructed Embassy on plot number 40. Here we see clearly the awkward shape of the plot on which Lutyens had to fit the Embassy and the garden. Later on, the British government purchased plots 38–9 allowing for a larger garden and, later still, plots 43–5 and 37, which provided land for the construction of the New Chancery building in the late 1950s.

Building a New Embassy 1925-30

Finding the Architect

Harry Wardman had come to the United States in 1889 as a seventeen-year-old carpenter from England with seven shillings in his pocket. From this inauspicious start, he established himself as the most successful property developer in Washington, capitalising on the rapid expansion of the city and the post-war boom in prices. He waxed lyrical to Howard about his plot: 'this property is situated on Massachusetts Avenue, at a very high point, overlooking the city, which is undoubtedly the best residential setting in the city of Washington ... I, myself, compare this Avenue with the Champs-Élysées in Paris'. So keen was Wardman to clinch the deal, he was willing to discount heavily, offering his land for $210,000, with the sweetener that he would buy the current embassy site for $450,000.[1] He even agreed to allow the British to remain in the Connecticut Avenue Embassy for three years while the new Embassy was being built. Contracts with Wardman were duly signed in the spring of 1925.

The Champs-Élysées the site was not. The area was separated from the centre of Washington by the deep gorge of Rock Creek Park. Only the construction of a bridge over the creek in 1901 had made the area easily accessible. There was little other civilisation nearby, with the exception of the Naval Observatory to the immediate north, which had moved there from Foggy Bottom in 1893.

At only four acres, the site was cramped. In addition to a double slope, upwards with the road and away from the road, the land available, marked plot 40 on the map opposite, was a very odd shape. As the map illustrates, the plot came with a relatively thin access strip to Massachusetts Avenue, but then broadened out the further it got from the road. The site was variously described as being in the shape of an inverted capital P, or a triangle on a narrow stand. This inauspicious piece of land would require a very special architect, with unusual technical mastery on top of artistic distinction.

The selection of architect fell to Lionel Earle in London. Visiting the United States in November 1924, he had talked to the distinguished American architect Cass Gilbert, who had recommended the commission be given to 'a first class British architect in conjunction with some reliable American architect'.[2] Earle had a deep admiration for the work of Edwin Lutyens, whose considerable body of work at home and growing portfolio abroad had already won great acclaim. He was impressed that the American Institute of Architects had awarded their prestigious Gold Medal to Lutyens, and argued that the British government 'could not pay a greater tribute to Washington than by selecting the artist they themselves had honoured'.[3] Lutyens' wife also happened to be Earle's cousin!

English culture and country life was particularly fashionable in the United States at the turn of the century and beyond. From the 1880s to the 1920s, country houses were being built across the United States, heavily modelled on English design. The life of the English aristocracy too held a particular fascination for many wealthy Americans, who dreamed of marrying their daughters into English nobility. The selection of Lutyens was thus particularly appropriate. A frisson of excitement rippled through American society at the news that the supreme architect of the English country house was to design an embassy in the nation's capital.

Lutyens the Man

Edwin Landseer Lutyens was born in March 1869, the eleventh of fourteen children. He was named after the celebrated painter of animals, Edwin Landseer, whom his father, an amateur artist, greatly admired. Because of poor health, Edwin, who preferred to be known as 'Ned' throughout his life, did not go away to boarding school, but studied at home. Whiling away the days at the family's large country house in the Surrey countryside, young Ned found plenty of time to wander the local lanes and pathways. He became enchanted by the local cottages and houses, churches and shops, many built from indigenous materials

LEFT Marsh Court (1901), built on a hill in rural Hampshire, is a transitional house between Lutyens' vernacular and Classical periods. Note the tall chimneys, which Lutyens uses less for functional reasons than aesthetic ones. As Gavin Stamp writes, Lutyens utilises chimneys 'carefully and precisely so as to hold a composition together'.[4] Lutyens designed his country houses for the affluent, with weekend entertaining a particular requirement.

BELOW Middleton Park (1938): a view of the south front. This house from late in Lutyens' career lacks the portico that graces the Residence but has many similar features including window shutters. Lutyens' houses often have asymmetrical interiors behind perfectly symmetrical facades.

FACING PAGE Lutyens in 1942, towards the end of his life. The architect is bent over one of his drawings, geometric instrument in his hand. His meticulous attention to detail and mathematical precision were enduring facets of his work.

including timber, brick, stone, tiling and thatch, and was captivated by the intricate skills of the local craftsmen. His preference for local materials can be traced to this period. He loved to make drawings on a sheet of glass, recording the perspectives he saw through it, using sharpened soap which he would later wash away. His profound understanding of perspective, and his love of long vistas, can also be dated to this period of his life.

In 1885, when still only fifteen, his parents sent him to the South Kensington School of Art, later the Royal College of Arts, to study architecture, in fulfilment of his dreams. While there, he became entranced by the work of William Morris (1834–96), John Ruskin (1819–1900) and Philip Webb (1831–1915). All three were leading figures in the 'Arts and Crafts Movement', at its height between 1860 and 1910. Its ideals of simple forms, love of natural materials, nostalgia and respect for craftsmanship

chimed deeply inside him. Although fiercely ambitious, Lutyens was not a natural student, and he left the College two years later. He became apprenticed to a successful London practice run by Ernest George, where he met a fellow architect who was to have a great impact on his life, Herbert Baker. Straining for greater freedom, Lutyens left in 1888, and, having secured his first commission at the age of just twenty, set up his office in Gray's Inn Square in London. His first task was to build a nine-bedroom house in Crooksbury, near Farnham in Surrey, for a friend of his parents. It was a promising start, but as the distinguished architectural historian Gavin Stamp put it, 'Lutyens' architecture did not really become remarkable until he began to work with a most remarkable client and collaborator, Gertrude Jekyll.'[4]

Lutyens always had a soft spot for powerful older women, an echo of his relationship with his mother, which was all the closer

for his not going away to school. Through the Crooksbury commission, Lutyens was to meet a woman twenty-five years his elder, who was living with her own mother in nearby Godalming. The lady, Gertrude Jekyll, had been creating a garden across the road from her family home and, in 1896, she invited the precocious young architect to design a house on it, to be called Munstead Wood. Jekyll was a painter whose failing eyesight had taken her in the direction of garden design. In the budding if still naïve architect Lutyens, she found the ideal professional partner, with whom she shared the same ethic of work and sense of aesthetic, where garden and house would work together in artistic harmony. Jekyll was to introduce Lutyens to many key figures in his life, including Edward Hudson, who in 1897 founded *Country Life*, the illustrated magazine which was to promote his work so enthusiastically.

Lutyens met another woman at the same time, Lady Emily Lytton, the daughter of the Earl of Lytton, Britain's first Viceroy to India. Lutyens fell hopelessly in love with her and, while wooing her, designed an elaborate miniature chest with drawers and secret compartments, one of which contained a drawing of a white house that he dreamed of building for her one day, in which they would live together. They married and had five children, but the white house was never realised. Professionally their marriage proved a significant boost to Lutyens, providing him with the connections he needed to develop his country house practice.

The period from 1897 to 1911 saw Lutyens at the height of his powers, designing country houses for newly affluent and cultured families, who wanted to live in elegant homes akin to the ancestral homes of the aristocracy. The romantic style and the 'Arts and Crafts Movement', were his first influences, as at Munstead Wood (1897) and nearby Orchards (1898). These are stylish vernacular properties that hug the lie of the land. With elegant gardens designed by Jekyll they drew on local materials and employed traditional craftsmen. Two houses, Marsh Court (1901) and Little Thakeham (1902), were designed during a transition period as Lutyens came under the influence of the Classical style, with Inigo Jones and Christopher Wren his new gurus. Indeed, with his love of punning, that so enchanted or antagonised people, he coined the term 'Wrennaissance' for his reworking of the Classical style. It came still more to the fore in a series of remarkable houses in the second half of this period in his life, including Folly Farm (1905–6), Great Maytham (1909) and The Salutations (1911), a house in Queen Anne style.

ABOVE An aerial photograph of the Residence in 1931.
LEFT Aerial view of the Viceroy's House, New Delhi. If you remove the dome, and add in the Portico from Washington, the exterior of the buildings would look not dissimilar. As in Washington, the geometric layout of the gardens demonstrates Lutyens' desire to create the equivalent of rooms outside, which would eventually develop shady areas offering relief from the punishing sun.
FACING PAGE Viceroy's House: the main entrance, 1931. Conscious of the heat, Lutyens designed the building with shaded walkways and few windows.

New Delhi

Towards the end of this fertile domestic period, Lutyens turned in a new direction, embarking on a project that was to prove flawed and troublesome, but also the seminal achievement of his life. In 1911, King George V announced that the capital city of India, then part of the British Empire, would move from Calcutta westwards, to New Delhi. Initially asked to advise on a location and plan for this entirely new city, Lutyens insisted on designing the principal government buildings himself, a mouth-watering project for any ambitious architect. Indeed, his assignment in New Delhi could be compared to the work of Wren, in rebuilding the City of London after the Great Fire of 1666, or Pierre Charles L'Enfant, appointed by President Washington, in 1791, to lay out the new capital of the United States.

The next twenty years were to enmesh Lutyens in endless bureaucratic and financial haggling, good preparation for his work on the Washington Embassy maybe, but which gave him little pleasure. The commission was also to sour his relationship with Herbert Baker, the fellow architect Lutyens called on to design the Secretariat buildings for civil servants, on either flank of Government House. Baker's two Secretariat buildings nonetheless complement Government House (renamed 'Viceroy's House' in 1929) perfectly, and add greatly to the majesty and presence of the new city. Lutyens designed a remarkable series of gardens behind the Viceroy's House, which terminate in the focal point of a circular water garden. In Washington he had much less space to play with, but he created similar geometrical patterns in the garden, above all in the circular steps.

Lutyens threw himself into the work in India, which included choosing the site for the twenty-five-mile-square new city. He was responsible for many key design decisions, including laying out its central administrative area, and some of the 'bungalows' (houses for government officials). But his principal task was the Viceroy's House. One of his many agonies came when the Viceroy, Lord Hardinge, cut his budget in half. Further heartache came when he realised that Baker's Secretariat buildings on Raisina summit would obscure the view of his own jewel on the approach from the two-mile processional route, named King's Way.

Lutyens was always a master synthesiser of styles, and in the Viceroy's House he blended Mogul and Hindu influences with European Classicism. Below is the grand East Front, with columns in Classical style; above them is a sharply pointed cornice, in Mogul style. The dominant feature is the rounded imperial dome, though notice too the roof pavilion, another Mogul feature. The structure, slightly larger than the Palace of Versailles outside Paris, contains some typical Lutyens features, several of which are found at the Washington Embassy, including inner courtyard and grand staircase, as well as an innovation, an entrance for cars and carriages underneath a building above. The work was to take Lutyens on long sea journeys to India for many winters until the building was eventually completed in 1929 and opened in 1931.

Memorials

The First World War (1914–18) led to work on New Delhi being suspended in 1917, but was to propel Lutyens in another new direction. In May 1917, the Imperial War Graves Commission (IWGC) was created to look after the graves of fallen soldiers from Britain and the Dominions. Lutyens saw this as his great opportunity to influence the style of memorials and cemeteries. That July, he travelled to France with a working party that included Herbert Baker and Charles Aitken, Director of the Tate

Gallery, to consider how to proceed. The experience moved him deeply: 'Each day we have long motor drives, being billeted in a chateau some way back from the front', he wrote to Emily, 'What humanity can endure and suffer is beyond belief.'[5] He came back with a clear idea of design – his ability to visualise three dimensional forms in his head was one of his great gifts. Baker had different ideas. Whereas he wanted Christian crosses on grave headstones, as the French were to have, Lutyens favoured solid gravestones, on whose uniform shape could be engraved a

Christian cross, or other religious symbol. Great solemn 'Stones of Remembrance', to be erected in the war cemeteries, were another Lutyens enthusiasm, and he prevailed successfully over Baker on most points of difference.

In 1919, Prime Minister Lloyd George invited Lutyens to Downing Street to ask him to design a monument which allied troops could march past on victory parade on 19 July. The Treaty of Versailles had been signed the previous month, and the parade, just ten days away, was to mark the official end of the war. Lutyens hurriedly erected a structure of wood and plaster in the middle of Whitehall, the street in London on which most government buildings were situated. He described his structure as a 'cenotaph', meaning empty tomb, a term he first encountered at Munstead Wood. The victory parade duly marched past it. So admired was the structure that Lutyens was invited to rebuild it in stone as a permanent memorial for Armistice Day, 11 November. The empty tomb lies at the top of the monument's pylon which, true to Classical style, has no straight lines; the verticals of the Cenotaph if projected up would meet 1,000 feet above ground, while the curve on the horizontals would meet 900 feet underground. Here Lutyens relied on his mastery of 'entasis', a technical term for the use of convexity in columns, conveying, when viewed at a distance, the impression of straight lines in a structure that would otherwise appear curved. The Cenotaph design was repeated in monuments elsewhere in Britain, notably in the port of Southampton, as well as in Hong Kong, Canada and New Zealand. He designed ninety further war memorials and cemeteries for the Imperial War Graves Commission.

The most physically impressive of Lutyens' war memorials abroad is the 'Memorial to the Missing of the Somme' in France, the largest British memorial in the world. Built on the ridge at Thiepval, which saw some of the most intense fighting of the whole Somme campaign (July-November 1916), it records the names of over 73,000 British soldiers who fell with no known grave. This monumental structure, with two heights of arches, offering differing perspectives from a series of angles, is built of red brick with limestone for the panels that bear the names of the fallen soldiers on sixteen piers. It can be seen for miles around, and was opened by the Prince of Wales (the future King Edward VIII, later Duke of Windsor) in 1932, in the presence of President Albert Lebrun of France. Thiepval is widely admired as a design of genius, though to some observers its stolid functionality lacks the artistry and poignancy of the Canadian memorial at Vimy Ridge, designed by Walter Allward and opened in 1936.

BELOW Every Remembrance Sunday, the monarch, the prime minister and the principal party leaders lay wreaths next to the Cenotaph, after two minutes' silence, while servicemen march past. *Passing of the Unknown Warrior in front of the Cenotaph, 11 November 1920*, oil on canvas by Frank O. Salisbury, 1920, in the Government Art Collection.

ABOVE The Thiepval Memorial, the Memorial to the Missing of the Somme. Lutyens faced a major logistical challenge in designing the monument because he needed space to carve the names of over seventy thousand soldiers, killed fighting on the Somme battlefields. The sixteen piers gave Lutyens potentially sixty-four surfaces on which names could be carved, with over a thousand on each panel. At the bottom of the great arch lies the Stone of Remembrance. Each cemetery with over a thousand graves (and also some with fewer) has such a stone bearing words chosen by Rudyard Kipling: 'Their Name Liveth For Evermore.'

LEFT This cemetery at Monchy in Northern France, one of Lutyens' finest, contains the graves of 581 men who fell in the First World War, fifty-eight of whom are unidentified. Notice the Classical arches and matching niche which reveal Lutyens' love of perspective. Echoes of this can be seen in the Main Corridor of the Residence. Notice the characteristic blend of brick and stone which we see repeated in the garden at the Residence.

Lutyens' Later Career

Lutyens had now become a figure of major national importance. In 1918, he was knighted, and in 1921 the Royal Institute of British Architects awarded him the prestigious Gold Medal, their highest honour. The 1920s saw Lutyens return to his traditional staple of country homes, such as Gledstone Hall (1923–6). Corporate work became productive now too, as at Britannic House (1920) and his Midland Banks, at Piccadilly (1922) and Poultry (1924), all in London. But for all his designs of banks and commercial buildings, churches and public buildings, it is for his country houses, and the Cenotaph, which first brought him fame, that he remains best known in Britain.

The 1930s saw him less in demand, as economies, fashion and advancing age acted against him, but he still became President of the Royal Academy on the eve of the Second World War. In 1938, working with his architect son, Robert, he designed Middleton Park in Oxfordshire, said to be the last great country house to be built in England during that period. Georgian in style, and with a dormered roof rising above stone cornices, it has many similarities to the Residence. Lutyens died in 1944. Reflecting the nation's esteem, he was honoured with a memorial in the crypt of St Paul's Cathedral, London.

Lutyens' achievement of some 550 buildings and structures was prodigious. Yet, even before his death, he had fallen out of vogue. Modernist architects, such as Le Corbusier and Frank Lloyd Wright, became the new masters of the age, whilst steel and concrete, two substances disparaged by Lutyens, became the materials of the post-war years. Many critics after 1945 regarded him as elitist and unimaginative, the servant of his clients – aristocrats, millionaires, banks and governments. Architectural historian Nicolas Pevsner, scandalously, said he had contributed nothing to the development of twentieth-century architecture, an opinion he later recanted. Wright too came to admire his work, as did Le Corbusier. Lutyens has now reclaimed his rightful place as the most important British architect of the first half of the twentieth century, and the equal of the two giants who dominated the final quarter of that century, Norman Foster and Richard Rogers.

Recurring Themes in Lutyens' Domestic Architecture

The time has now come to consider more precisely how Lutyens' earlier buildings might have shaped his design for the Washington Embassy. No papers survive recording the thinking behind Lutyens' design, but a study of his earlier work provides rich insights. Lutyens' trademark features include his generous use of space in hallways, staircases, landings, inner courtyards and corridors. His eye for detail is evident in the great attention he paid to garden vistas, to geometric designs and floor patterns, carving and friezes, fireplaces and mantelpieces, quirks and

architectural tricks, concealed guttering, graceful spiral stairs, to lighting fixtures and furniture designs, and to contrasting use of colour and natural materials.

The entrance corridor at the Viceroy's House recalls the Entry Hall for the Residence in Washington, with black-and-white patterned flooring, depth and perspective, and stone walls. But in New Delhi, Lutyens had greater height at his disposal, hence he was able to employ arches. Gledstone Hall, which was completed in 1926 as Lutyens was turning his mind to mastering the challenging site in Washington, is a remarkable precursor to

the Residence. The ground floor corridor bears striking similarities to the Main Corridor in the Residence, with great depth, the familiar black-and-white patterned flooring, and a series of receding arches framing the view.

Still more intriguing is the inspiration Lutyens may have derived from the work of Sir John Soane (1753–1837), the distinguished neoclassical architect, best known for the Bank of England in London. In the 1790s, Soane was often called upon to build or remodel the homes of the landed gentry. One of his designs was Tyringham Hall, where Lutyens was called in to work on the garden and create new pavilions in 1924, the year before he was given the Washington commission. He admired Soane, and no doubt spent much time wandering around the house absorbing the architect's work. Lutyens' design for a corridor beneath a dome, in the Temple of Music at Tyringham Hall, may well have inspired the design for the Main Corridor and Ballroom in the Washington Residence. Lutyens had used marble columns earlier, as at Heathcote in Yorkshire. But the way they are used both at Tyringham and in the Residence to define the shape of a room is distinctive.

Another style of corridor can be seen at Castle Drogo on Dartmoor in Devon, a granite castle which took nearly twenty years to complete. Lutyens' love of perspective and depth, and having the corridor opening out onto spaces on either side was a device he was to use again in Washington. At Gledstone Hall he built columns on solid plinths, which have echoes in his design for the Embassy. He also devised a prominent loggia, with considerable covered outdoor space, which was much in his mind when he designed the Portico, concurrently, for the Residence.

Lutyens' Portico at the Washington Embassy is dominated by Ionic columns arranged in rows of four and two, with the British royal coat of arms prominently carved in the pediment. The façade at Gledstone (facing page), Lutyens' only house with a projecting portico, displays a comparable arrangement of columns, with a prominent emblem carved in its pediment. Both porticos owe much to Andrea Palladio, the sixteenth-century Italian architect. While the similarity between both Lutyens' buildings is striking, the use of load-bearing columns was common in American Colonial architecture. Columns are also employed prominently at the White House. So, while Gledstone was an important precursor, it is likely that Lutyens would have given the Residence a portico even without his earlier work to draw on.

Lutyens' playful love of staircases can be seen below. Initially, under the influence of the 'Arts and Crafts Movement', he tended

FACING PAGE, LEFT The dramatic circular staircase at 42 Cheyne Walk, designed by Lutyens for Guy Liddell and his wife, 1933: 'one of the elements of Beauty is Surprise', Lutyens once said.

FACING PAGE, RIGHT The staircase at Gledstone Hall is unusual in Lutyens' use of alternating treads of black and white marble to complement the overall scheme of the house, which uses different colours of stone – similar to his floor patterns – to make an architectural statement. Note the railing, which has a distinct resemblance to the railing at the Residence. Lutyens lavished a great amount of the space available to him on his staircases, which were often of double height, as we see here.

ABOVE The south east elevation at Gledstone Hall, the only other major building that Lutyens designed with a portico, was influenced by the work of Palladio. Notice the elaborately carved coat of arms in the pediment.

to build them of wood, but later turned to marble and limestone. He had a great fondness for spiral staircases, which appealed to his love of geometry and replication of patterns that occur in nature. One of his most impressive spiral staircases was at Midland Bank, Poultry, and he repeated the formula at 42 Cheyne Walk (1930), a house on the River Thames, now sadly demolished. The spiral staircase originates in a well with his familiar star pattern design. The staircase has a breathtaking sweep and employs acute mathematical and geometric patterning. At Washington, he was able to build both a grand sweeping staircase, as well as a spiral staircase. No one looking at these photographs can dispute they are looking at the work of a master.

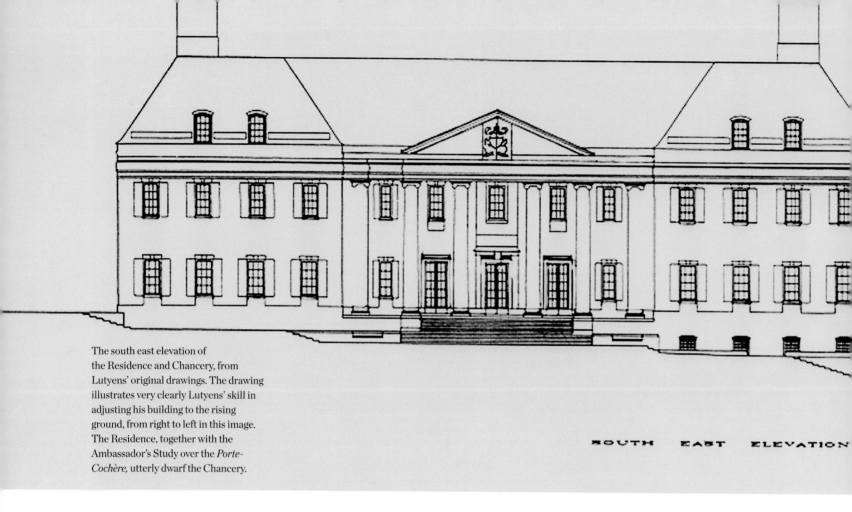

The south east elevation of the Residence and Chancery, from Lutyens' original drawings. The drawing illustrates very clearly Lutyens' skill in adjusting his building to the rising ground, from right to left in this image. The Residence, together with the Ambassador's Study over the *Porte-Cochère,* utterly dwarf the Chancery.

SOUTH   EAST   ELEVATION

ABOVE The north portico of the White House with two carefully manicured laurel trees, which are emulated under the Portico at the Residence today. How significantly the White House influenced Lutyens' decision to include a colonnade and portico, a design element he included very rarely in his buildings, is impossible to say.

Finding the Design

Lutyens enjoyed his first visit to the United States in April 1925 to collect his gold medal in New York from the American Institute of Architects. On the boat back to England, he busied himself sketching designs for the Embassy. In May, he called on Earle in Whitehall, and described excitedly the design that had now taken shape in his head. 'On the Massachusetts Avenue side, he will make a forecourt of the Chancery buildings, with the Embassy standing behind on the higher ground.'[6] Satisfied, Earle wrote to the Treasury requesting that Lutyens be officially appointed. He did, however, sound a note of caution for the controllers of the public purse: 'the scheme will prove more expensive than we had hoped, but this cannot be helped; we must not spoil the ship for a half-penny worth of tar'.[7]

Earle met Ambassador Howard to talk it through, and wrote to Lutyens noting that whereas the ambassador was in broad agreement with the plans, he felt the artistic style envisaged for the Chancery should be toned down, considering their 'architectural character' extravagant.[8] Howard growled too about garage space for his cars. But their relationship was still friendly and Lutyens wrote him a cordial letter in early July. 'I'm here doing graves in France – and the magnitude of that host of boys that died so fearfully still quickens the senses of unspeakable deso-

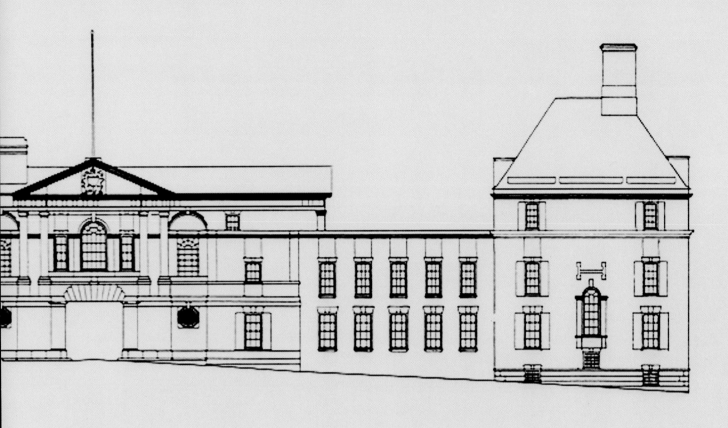

lation.' Busy though Lutyens was with the Imperial War Graves Commission, and New Delhi, he sought to reassure Howard that he remained focused. 'The Embassy is mostly in my mind' though 'it is not yet completely laid to paper'. He promised to send his latest sketches: 'it is myself that alone can do them'.[9]

The Treasury assented to the appointment of Lutyens, but with qualms: 'I believe his reputation is that of an extremely extravagant architect who doesn't care what he lets his client in for', wrote a senior Treasury official to Earle in June 1925.[10] It was concerned about repaying the huge debt to the United States that had been accumulated during the First World War. Efforts to keep government spending to an absolute minimum led to months of battles over estimates and re-estimates, which ground Lutyens down, and took away much of his pleasure in the commission.

Lutyens too was under pressure to complete his work in New Delhi, and he spent much of the winter of 1925–6 in India. In May 1926, he presented the Office of Works with his fourth Washington scheme, consisting of sketch plans and elevations to sixteenth-inch scale. They met with approval, 'the scheme as a whole has ... great charm and character, as was, of course, expected from Sir Edwin Lutyens', although concerns once again emerged over whether the design was achievable for the £165,000 allotted. Lutyens nevertheless was given a green

light to produce proper working drawings, and he assigned six assistants to the task – 'all working late'.[11] Still further cuts were demanded, some of which led to months of argument and recrimination, notably the loss of a passenger lift, a laundry and a cottage for the ambassador's chauffeur.

Only on 13 June 1927 was Lutyens' contract finally agreed and signed: his personal commission would be an exceptional 6 percent on cost, and he would be paid an additional ten guineas a day for time spent in Washington and five guineas a day for time crossing the Atlantic. Lutyens was to be assisted by a local architect, Frederick H. Brooke, based in Washington. The endless battles over money aggravated Lutyens exceedingly. In February 1927, he wrote, 'I may be going to America. But I must wait for the estimates – the Ambassador fusses and wants me out there [but it] is an impossible proposition.'[12] In September, the Treasury finally authorised, very grudgingly, an expenditure of £193,000 (which eventually rose to £197,680 with an additional £7,000 on furniture). 'My dear Ned,' Earle wrote to Lutyens in India, 'I am very anxious to see you at the earliest opportunity ... Esme Howard is getting extremely restive at the long and serious delay in making a start on this building, and we must strain every nerve to get competitive tenders for the whole job at the earliest date possible.'[13]

LEFT The Chancery nearing completion, taken some weeks after the earlier photograph of the Embassy under construction on page 36.
BELOW Sir Esme Howard at the ceremony laying the cornerstone for the Embassy on 3 June 1928. Notice the rough uneven land on which the Embassy was being built.
FACING PAGE Sir Ronald Lindsay, ambassador, 1930–9, sitting at his desk.

Construction Trials and Tribulations

Construction eventually got underway on 3 January 1928 amidst great optimism, and a commemorative cornerstone was laid by Howard on 3 June, King George V's birthday. Inside was placed a copper box containing plans of the Embassy and a document signed by Howard, whose dream the whole project had been.

Construction of large buildings is rarely straightforward and the work took longer than expected. From the start, America's powerful construction labour unions took exception to Harry Wardman, whom they considered hostile to their interests. The deteriorating American economy was a still greater problem. The Wall Street Crash in October 1929 almost finished Wardman. Already running six months late, he announced in the winter of 1929–30 that he could no longer afford temporary heating to dry out the Embassy structure. By the summer of 1930, he complained to Lutyens about 'this terrible business depression that makes it almost impossible for me to carry on my business'.[14] By that October he was unable to pay his subcontractors: he had 'no resources, an unknown amount of debt, no organisation, no staff, no credit'.[15] The Office of Works in London had to provide subsidies to prevent work stopping altogether.

Throughout the building process, Howard bombarded London with letters of complaint and personal suggestions. His insistence on a larger Chancery was finally accepted, leading to an additional floor on both wings at the front of the building. Some believe this made for a more satisfying presence facing Massachusetts Avenue, though the extra space created soon became woefully inadequate for the expanding Embassy. Many of his ideas created resentment and more paperwork, even when they were well grounded.

The size of the garage was a running sore. 'It is another case of "that damned fellow Lutyens" not making his rooms large enough', expostulated Howard in a letter to Earle in December 1928. 'My chauffeur, Hadley, whom you know, and who if nothing is not sarcastic, said that he thought that ... Sir Edwin ... must have been dreaming of Baby Austins.'[16] Howard became even more dyspeptic in 1929. By the middle of the year, the need for a central staircase in the Chancery became an obsession, because the ambassador feared that staff would waste too much time walking along corridors: 'this idea that time is money, of course would not appeal to Lutyens', he jabbed.[17] In one of his final letters, Howard was even cross about one of Lutyens' major architectural coups, the Ambassador's Study forming a bridge over the entrance porch: 'I dislike the entrance, with the Bridge of Sighs hanging oppressively over one's head as one comes in and I dislike also the view into the basement as one enters which ... resembles the entrance to a tube station or a mortuary chapel.'[18]

Long before he left Washington in 1930, Howard had been thoroughly ground down by the whole long process: 'much as I should have liked to have been the first [to enter the new Embassy] I very much doubt that I shall be able to do so. This place, as you know, is a pretty considerable strain, and I am beginning to feel that I am getting old', he wrote.[19]

Sir Ronald Lindsay, his successor, was one of the high fliers in the British Foreign Office. It was a mark of the importance London attached to relations with Washington that such a man was sent out, at the age of fifty-two, to open the new Embassy. He was married to an exceptional American lady, Elizabeth Sherman Hoyt, who was to make a great impact on the new property, above all on its garden. The building was nearing completion, but despite two visits from Lutyens in October 1928 and September 1929, and extensive work on the ground by Brooke, the local architect, much remained to be done. The Lindsays thus decided to stay at the Mayflower Hotel until ready to move in.

If Lutyens and Earle thought Howard had given them a hard time, they had not yet experienced Lindsay. 'I don't think it fair that we should have to move into this new house with any one of these deficiencies unremedied', Lindsay wrote in April 1930, enclosing a list of eleven points he had drawn up with Brooke. These included doors which were 'undignified and unsafe' and problems with 'hot water pipes which must be remedied at once'.[20] Concerned, Earle visited the site again, as did Lutyens in May 1930. The latter was irritated: 'they are perfectly terrible at getting things finished – and the Office of Works' official stringency as regards funds has led to a sort of mental paralysis ... everyone is so tired of correspondence and estimating and reestimating that they are dog tired of the job – it is a pity to spoil a good building'.[21]

Chancery staff moved into the unfinished building on 30 May. What they found made Lindsay positively angry. 'It makes me ask myself whether anything that we said to you when you were out here had any effect', he wrote to Earle, enclosing again his list of eleven complaints from April: 'only two have been rectified'. In sterner vein: 'The more I think of it all, the more convinced I am that we are being treated with extreme unfairness ... do you really think it is our duty to put up with such indignity? Because, frankly, I can't think so myself.'[22]

Three days later, on 5 June, the Lindsays moved into the Residence. Later that month, Lady Lindsay wrote a respectful letter, reminding Lutyens that he had requested she send him a diary of problems she encountered: 'on your head be it!' she wrote: 'It is, I am afraid, a rather purple document.' She was careful to praise Lutyens: 'the beauty of [the building's] exterior increases daily', but added that 'the interior would have been equally wonderful if only someone had seen to the material and the workmanship ... At the moment we are dizzy with confusion, deafened by noise, poisoned by flies, exasperated by ineptitudes and overrun by rats.'[23] The 'diary' went on for many pages. On 7 June, for example: 'this morning, after a sleepless night, when I tried to leave my bedroom, I could not get out as the door had jammed during the damp night'.[24]

On the same day, she wrote to Earle to say that 'the whole of Washington is anxiously waiting to see this building'. The Lindsays wanted to be entertaining by September or October 1930 at the latest, so a plethora of faults required immediate attention. Some of the problems were undoubtedly due to Wardman, who was running out of money to pay workmen. Supply problems, especially of special, small, hand-finished bricks from Virginia used in the building, also did not help. Nor did the delay in getting the drawings from Lutyens' office in London to Washington. The Office of Works was by now deeply concerned. An internal memo recorded: 'if the criticisms made by Lady Lindsay in her diary are true, the position ... is a very serious one'. The document also expressed surprise that the defects were 'not discovered by Edwin Lutyens during his recent visit to Washington'.[25] In response, Lutyens sent one of his staff across to Washington, who replaced the defective ballroom floor, the door and window openings and fitted fly screens to the windows.

The strain proved too much for Lady Lindsay, who was taken ill and went off to Long Island to recover. During her prolonged absence, until March 1931, the building finally came together. On her return she wrote to Earle – the unsung hero of the entire project – to say: 'I am just back after a weary absence of seven months ... I am more and more amazed at your foresight and imagination at having selected this particular site ... the embassy is extraordinary beautiful, both outside and in ... everyone who comes to see it is struck with its beauty and dignity ... here you have surpassed even yourself, and I shall never be content until you and Sir Edwin have seen this place in its finished form and to have realised the beauty of your joint accomplishment.'[26]

A letter the same day to Lutyens was embarrassingly effusive, 'at long last I am back in this lovely house, it is beautiful beyond compare, and we are happy in every corner of it. Thank you a thousand times. We are your slaves'.[27]

LEFT The front of Monticello, the home of President Thomas Jefferson, near Charlottesville, Virginia. Lutyens would very likely have been influenced by this iconic building. As at the White House, the portico at Monticello may have influenced Lutyens' design, although the precise impact is impossible to quantify.
FACING PAGE The south facing wall of the Chancery, designed as Lutyens drew it on page 51, with the flourishes above the window and the blend of small bricks from Virginia and stone. Lutyens' inventive playfulness with Classical style may have flowed, in part, from his lack of rigorous academic training.

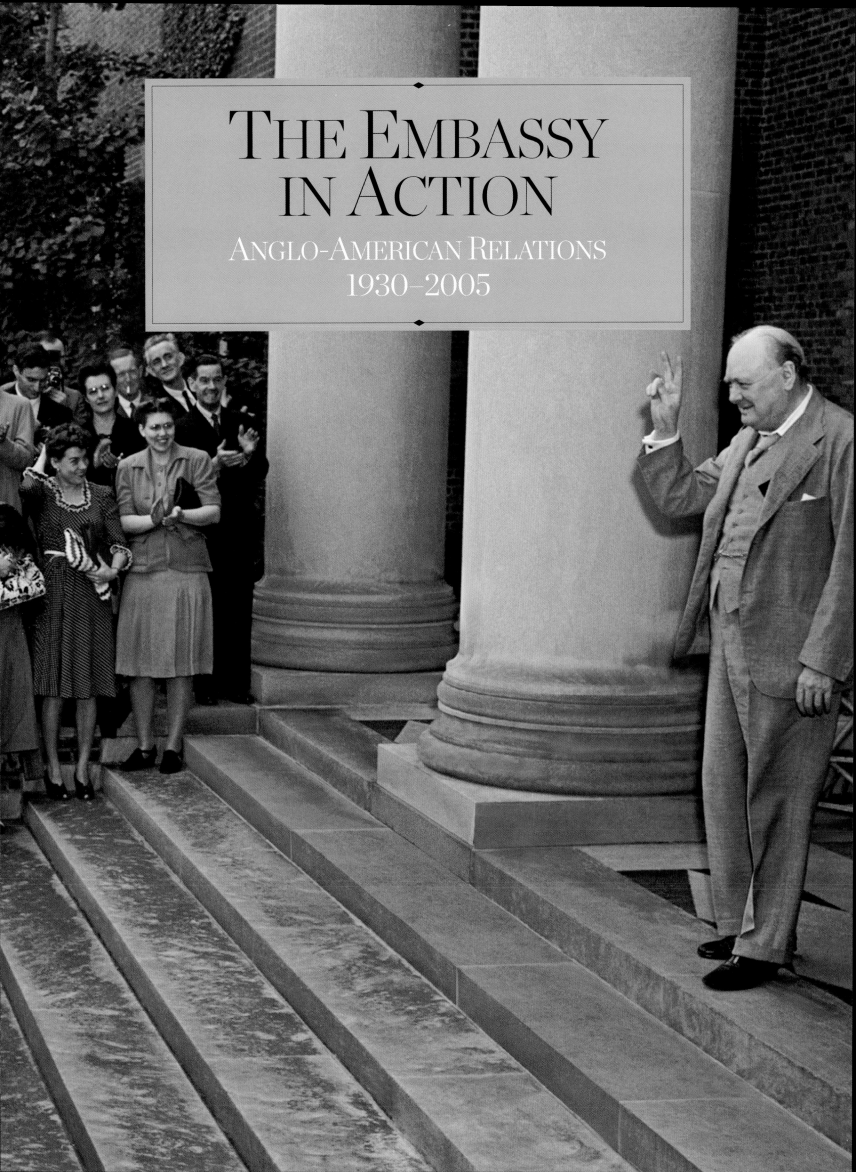

The Embassy in Action

Anglo-American Relations 1930–2005

PAGES 56–7 The prime minister, Winston Churchill, stands under the Portico to address enthused members of the Embassy staff in May 1943. Churchill's affection for the Residence, which he visited regularly, lingers to this day amongst those living and working in the building.

ABOVE In October 1929, Ramsay MacDonald became the first British prime minister to visit the United States. Here, with Secretary of State Henry L. Stimson, he greets crowds of well-wishers in New York City.

FACING PAGE Ramsay MacDonald returned to the United States in April 1933 and met the new president, Franklin D. Roosevelt. Arriving here at the White House, Roosevelt shakes MacDonald's hand. To MacDonald's right are his daughter, Ishbel, and First Lady Eleanor Roosevelt.

Diplomatic History 1930–2005

Anglo-American Relations in the 1930s

The inauguration of the new Embassy appeared, at first, to come at a promising time for Anglo-American relations. Stanley Baldwin, David Lloyd George's successor as prime minister, had decided in 1929 to go to Washington in person to improve the state of the relationship. But Baldwin's defeat in the general election of that May meant that his successor, Ramsay MacDonald, became the first prime minister to cross the Atlantic, which he did by boat in October 1929.

MacDonald's visit proved a considerable success. His face-to-face encounter with President Hoover helped usher in an age in which personal relationships between presidents and prime ministers would become key variables in shaping the Anglo-American partnership. In this case, MacDonald was eager to ease tension over the relative size and strength of the British and American navies. Herbert Hoover and his secretary of state, Henry Stimson, agreed and were both wedded to improving the relationship with London. The work of the trip bore fruit in the London Naval Conference of June 1930, which brought to an end twelve years of intense naval rivalry between Britain and America.

Despite this promising start, the 1930s were not an easy time for Anglo-American relations. The onset of the Great Depression only exacerbated economic rivalry and rancour between the two nations. In November 1932, Franklin D. Roosevelt (FDR) was elected president pledging to focus intently on domestic policy and economy recovery. This did nothing to improve the relationship with Britain. As the decade unfolded, British despair at the unwillingness of the United States to use its vast resources to help shape the deteriorating international position was the principal source of aggravation.

While the British government of Neville Chamberlain actively appeased growing Nazi aggression, America seemed determined to remain uninvolved. Although Roosevelt was, at heart, an

anglophile and a Wilsonian internationalist, his hands were tied by the predominance of isolationist sentiment at home. From the late 1930s, however, particularly after the Munich Crisis in September 1938, Roosevelt felt able to act. The navies of both countries began to work together from late 1937, planning a response to the German and Japanese naval threat. Over the next two years, spurred by the events in Europe, the reserve of the US establishment towards the British progressively yielded. The growing warmth of the relationship was confirmed by the invitation to George VI to visit the United States in the summer of 1939.

BUCKINGHAM PALACE

3rd. November, 1938.

My dear President Roosevelt

I have now been able to give further thought to
the plans for my visit to Canada, with their special bearing
on your very kind invitation to The Queen and myself to stay
with you in the United States. I am happy to say that the
way now seems clear for me to gratify my wish and accept
this invitation, which I do with the utmost pleasure.

As it is undesirable for me, in these disturbed
days, to be too long absent from the United Kingdom, and
as I shall have so large a programme to carry out in Canada,
I fear that it may not be possible for me to avail myself of
your hospitality for more than four days. You will, I feel
sure, agree that it is too early yet to discuss details, but
it may not be easy for me to come to the United States until
nearly the end of my Canadian Tour, that is to say about the

VISIT OF GEORGE VI

In June 1939, George VI became the first ruling British monarch to visit the United States. At the King's request, Lindsay had delayed his departure as ambassador for the event: 'I do feel that the best we can do for Anglo-American relations is to assure, by all the means we can, the success of the royal visit' Lord Halifax, the foreign secretary, wrote to the prime minister, 'and I think it very desirable therefore that Lindsay, with his long experience and great knowledge should be on hand to advise.'[a] As war in Europe loomed, the visit aimed to build goodwill amongst the American people, but it was not intended to be overtly political. At first, Halifax hoped to accompany the King, but the very idea led Roosevelt to 'grimace', warning that it would 'excite a lot of talk about an alliance'.[b] At Lindsay's urging, Halifax agreed to stay away.

The King and Queen were to arrive in America by train from Canada on 7 June. The visit proper would begin in Washington, with the couple staying at the White House. The schedule for their four-day visit included stops at the Capitol, Mount Vernon, New York and a picnic at Hyde Park, Roosevelt's country retreat. In what became Washington's most sought-after social event in living memory, the Embassy also planned a royal garden party for 8 June. In a royal schedule of exclusive lunches and dinners, the garden party at the Residence was the only event open, at least in theory, to a broader audience. The problem was that demand vastly outstripped supply. Americans, by their thousands, wanted to meet the King and Queen and many wrote to Lady Lindsay demanding an invitation. Fearing a backlash against Britain from the uninvited hordes, she 'decided to deliberately put my own neck out for the blows' and assumed full responsibility for the guest list. The result was painful. 'I have been subjected to personal attacks in ... the yellow Press of America, and I confess I quiver under it.'[c]

FACING PAGE George VI writes to accept, in principle, Roosevelt's invitation to visit the United States. In later correspondence, he extended a personal invitation for Roosevelt to dine at the Residence during his trip. Although the president rarely dined out at embassies, he accepted immediately.

ABOVE, LEFT George VI and President Roosevelt during the royal procession through Washington, on 8 June 1939. By the end of the visit, the two leaders had struck up a rapport.

ABOVE, RIGHT Accompanied by the ambassador, Sir Ronald Lindsay, George VI prepares to mingle with guests at the Embassy garden party on 8 June 1939. They are walking across the Lower Terrace immediately adjacent to the steps leading to the Portico.

PAGES 62–3 Queen Elizabeth and Eleanor Roosevelt turn heads during a royal procession through Washington on 8 June 1939.

ABOVE Standing under the Portico,
the King and Queen are presented
to the large crowd gathered
in the garden below.

LEFT Those lucky enough to attend
the garden party had to contend
with questions of proper dress and
etiquette. Hats for the ladies went
without saying, and Lady Lindsay
suggested floor-length dresses.
She was reluctant to address
the thorny question of whether
Americans should curtsy or bow but
suggested it would be polite to do so.

FACING PAGE George VI and the great
anglophile J. Pierpont Morgan, Jr,
enjoy tea together on the Terrace.

PAGES 66–7 Lutyens' Portico provides an
elegant backdrop for America's élite
to mingle as a very select group
prepares to meet the royal couple.

The press, many of whom resented not being invited themselves, quizzed Lady Lindsay mercilessly on controversial questions of etiquette – even if not a British subject, when meeting the Royals one might bend a knee 'as a matter of politeness', she suggested – and on the non-official guests, whom Lindsay revealed had been drawn from the exclusive 'Social Register'. With the media furore growing, the ambassador himself held a press conference, something he had avoided for the past nine years. Unfortunately he did little better than his wife. Asked why more 'average Americans' had not been invited, he replied: 'There's such an awful lot of them.'[d] This was a struggle the Lindsays could not win, but several hundred new names were added, bringing the total number of guests to around one thousand five hundred.

On 8 June, following the etiquette for Buckingham Palace garden parties, the Embassy gates opened at 4 p.m. Strawberries and cream were served with sandwiches and white wine punch. The royal party arrived around 5:20 p.m. to be greeted by Vice President and Mrs John Nance Garner and other political notables on the Terrace. Shortly afterwards, the Royals walked down into the garden. The King, 'in a superbly fitted dark cutaway with dark trousers', was escorted by the ambassador while The Queen, in a gown of 'white net with embroidered panels edged with ruffles', was guided by Lady Lindsay.[e] Most guests bowed, curtsied or shook hands. One Texan congressman deliberately broke protocol, shouting 'Hi-ya, Cousin George!', but the King only smiled.

After a few drops of rain, the Royals retreated to the Terrace for tea with an exclusive few, including J. Pierpont Morgan, Jr, and Edith Wilson, widow of President Woodrow Wilson, and John D. Rockefeller. The white-helmeted naval band then struck up 'God Save the King' and the Royals left to cheers. The garden party, like the rest of the visit, ended in triumph. The King and Queen's easy grace had won many admirers and Britain's stock rose accordingly.

At War:
Forging the 'Special Relationship' 1939–45

BY 1939, BRITAIN AND AMERICA WERE DRAWING CLOSER together. Britain had moved away from appeasement and Roosevelt had produced plans for rearmament. For all this, the Nazis posed a far more direct threat to British interests and the United States remained firmly wedded to a policy of neutrality. Britain and America were now friends, but not yet partners.

Tackling American Neutrality

The appointment of Philip Kerr, 11th Marquess of Lothian, to succeed Lindsay as ambassador was designed to deepen UK-US ties, but proved controversial. 'I have been conscious that in the limited Foreign Office circle which knows of his selection, there are misgivings of a more or less pronounced nature, which go beyond the Foreign Office natural preference for a career man speaking the Foreign Office jargon and knowing all the ropes', the outgoing Lindsay wrote to Lord Halifax in March.[1]

This much was true. Lord Lothian was a journalist and a politician rather than a career diplomat. He had also previously been a full-throated supporter of appeasement, although had since rejected this approach. But, for a salary of £2,500 (plus an outfit allowance of £800), he brought a deep understanding of America, which he had visited regularly as a journalist. Writing to Halifax, Lindsay stressed that he did not share the misgivings about Lothian. He had met 'a tremendous number' of Americans 'and they: 'like him ... he has the knack of moving about a great deal in an unobtrusive (not a secret or surreptitious) manner. This is a valuable quality for a British ambassador in America ... If he has to follow a bolder and more forward line of policy than I have, he will be wary enough to begin cautiously and sensitive enough to become aware of possible danger'.[2] As Lothian arrived in Washington that August, the increasingly desperate situation in Europe meant that a 'bolder and more forward line of policy' was inevitable.

On 31 August 1939, Germany invaded Poland. Three days later Britain and France declared war. America, shielded by three thousand miles of Atlantic Ocean, remained isolationist.

Under the amended Neutrality Act (1937), the United States could trade with Britain only on a 'cash-and-carry' basis, with the sale of arms forbidden.

Having met with FDR on 1 September, Lothian reported that 'the President felt very badly about having to issue his neutrality proclamation when every fibre of his being sympathises with Britain and France'. Repealing the act, he said, would require shifting public opinion.[3] Lothian now worked tirelessly to change perceptions, delivering personally crafted speeches to influential audiences. 'I can imagine what my speeches would have been like if they had first been minuted by all the veterans of the Foreign Office at home!' he wrote to Halifax. 'Yet they have all been a success here because I have felt that I knew the American mind well enough to be quite frank.'[4]

Slowly – very slowly – opinions in the United States began to change. On 4 November, Congress ended the arms embargo. Of greater significance was the 'Destroyers for Bases' agreement concluded in September 1940. Britain now granted the United States ninety-nine-year leases to establish military bases in Canada and the West Indies in exchange for fifty older (and somewhat decrepit) US vessels. In material terms it was a poor deal for Britain, but symbolically it was invaluable. It brought America closer to the British cause.

Lothian, of course, cannot claim all the credit. Becoming prime minister in May 1940, Winston Churchill brought his own persuasive gifts to bear. With the fall of France in June and the Blitz that September, US sympathy for Britain's plight grew. The possibility of Britain's powerful navy falling into German hands also weighed heavily. All this reinforced Lothian's message, which infuriated the isolationists. One activist wrote to the State Department, in September 1940, as follows: 'If we don't stop letting Lord Lothian direct our foreign policy, he is going to get us into war. That is his business. He is looking out for the interests of Britain and NOT THAT OF THE UNITED STATES. I would appreciate an American policy by OUR state [sic] Dept.'[5]

FACING PAGE Lord Lothian, in full ambassadorial regalia, leaves the Residence for a diplomatic reception at the White House three-and-a-half months after the outbreak of war in Europe. According to US diplomat William Bullitt, President Roosevelt liked Lothian and 'was always pleased to see him'.

CHURCHILL AT THE EMBASSY

From 1900 to 1959, Winston Churchill visited Washington thirteen times and, in the 1940s and 1950s, he became a regular figure at the Residence. During the Second World War, he preferred to sleep at the White House, keeping close to Roosevelt, but held meetings, lunches and dinners at the Residence and stayed there on occasion. These visits offered a real morale boost for Embassy staff. Betty Giles, a young cypher clerk, recalled Churchill standing on a table at a Christmas party in 1941: 'I was thrilled to see him looking so much younger than I expected – and so well too. He gazed down on us with a fat fatherly smile on his face ... How he was guarded – far more than the Windsors – but of course he's much more valuable.'[a]

Winston Churchill, no longer
prime minister, visits the Residence
in March 1949 and is greeted by
Embassy staff and an appropriately
enthusiastic pet dog. Churchill used
a brief meeting with President Harry
Truman to urge the president to
declare publicly that he would use the
atomic bomb to defend democratic
values if needed. Following the
creation of NATO in April, Truman
obliged; In 1959, Churchill visited
Washington for the last time. Here,
Vice President Richard Nixon and
President Dwight Eisenhower flank
Churchill as they honour him over
dinner at the Residence on 7 May
1959; Although Churchill was never
as close to Truman as he was to
Roosevelt, he was sad to see Truman
leave office in 1953. Now prime
minister again, Churchill visited
Washington that January. Here, he
pins a flower on Truman's coat at the
Residence on 8 January 1953.

ABOVE Embassy staff applaud Winston
Churchill as he leaves the Residence
for a meeting with President Truman
at the White House in January 1952.
RIGHT Churchill addresses Embassy
staff and War Office employees from
under the Portico, following lunch
at the Residence on 22 May 1943.
His surprise visit, and news of German
collapse in North Africa, boosted
morale in Washington.

Lothian's most enduring personal contribution to UK-US diplomacy came towards the end of his tenure. By November 1940, Britain's ability to purchase goods from the United States was almost exhausted. This was a hugely sensitive area, because the administration had always stressed the dollar benefits of selling to Britain. Speaking off the cuff, Lothian blew this argument sky high: 'Well, boys,' he said to the press, 'Britain's broke; it's your money we want.'[6] Lothian's blunt speaking infuriated the administration, but it helped prepare the ground for the next crucial step in UK-US collaboration, Lend-Lease.

On Sunday 8 December 1940, Lothian was taken ill. Three days later he died. As a Christian Scientist, Lothian had refused orthodox treatment, much to the consternation of Embassy officials. 'It was Lord Lothian's wish to have the form of treatment which he chose', wrote Nevile Butler, his deputy. 'He was weak and drowsy during the three days, and sometimes rambled, but on each day he talked lucidly and there was no question of his wishing a change of treatment.'[7] An official funeral followed. On 17 December, Lothian's body was loaded onto a gun carriage outside the Residence and drawn by six horses to the Cathedral of St Peter and St Paul. Demonstrating the affection in which Lothian was held, crowds lined the streets, many openly weeping. Lothian's ashes were stored at Arlington ceremony and repatriated to the UK at the end of the war.

LEFT The Duke and Duchess of Windsor, visiting Washington in September 1941, pause on the Residence's Grand Staircase. Suspected of pro-Nazi sympathies, the Duke was sent off to be Governor of the Bahamas from August 1940 until almost the end of the war. It was not a posting he enjoyed and he and the Duchess savoured their chance to visit the United States.

Lord Halifax

Edward Frederick Lindley Wood, 3rd Viscount and 1st Earl of Halifax, was not Churchill's first choice to replace Lothian. Initially, Churchill had wanted former prime minister Lloyd George and proposed him to Roosevelt. But after Lloyd George turned down the job, Churchill seized upon Halifax, his foreign secretary and rival for the prime ministership after Neville Chamberlain's resignation that May. To his private secretary, Churchill suggested this was a 'glorious opportunity' for Halifax: 'he would never live down the reputation for appeasement which he and the F.O. (Foreign Office) had won themselves here. He had no future in this country'.[a] Sending the foreign secretary as ambassador would illustrate just how important Britain considered UK-US relations. Churchill was also happy to exile a possible future rival to his leadership.

NEW BRITISH AMBASSADOR

FEBRUARY 10, 1941   10 CENTS
YEARLY SUBSCRIPTION $4.50

Halifax, however, was horrified. An aristocrat, following a family tradition of public service, he had thrived in imperial India in the grand post of Viceroy. The brash equality of America was something very different, and particularly abhorrent to the British upper classes. 'I have never liked Americans, except odd ones', Halifax told Stanley Baldwin, who had been Britain's prime minister until 1937. 'In the mass I have always found them dreadful.'[b] Desperately he tried to dissuade the prime minister, as did Lady Halifax. But Churchill was immovable. And so Halifax gave way: 'I still cannot help thinking that Winston has made a mistake', he wrote in his diary.[c]

On 24 January 1941, Halifax arrived at Chesapeake Bay on board the brand new *King George V* battleship. Roosevelt broke diplomatic precedent and sailed out to meet him on his yacht, *Potomac*. Yet from this promising start flowed only disappointment. Roosevelt and Churchill continued to communicate directly without, for a while, even providing Halifax with copies of their correspondence. 'All business in the U.S.A. is now transacted by telephoning and "popping in", both of which H can't abide', noted one official.[d] Halifax failed to understand the importance of social contacts in lubricating the American system and complained to Churchill that 'a great deal of what we try to do from the outside seems like hitting wads of cotton wool'.[e]

Recognising his shortcomings, Halifax took advice from his wife and his cousin, Angus McDonnell, who had lived in America for many years. McDonnell, who joined Halifax's staff, was now charged with what he called 'de-icing Edward'. This proved a great success. McDonnell soon engineered a breakthrough in relations with Colonel Edwin 'Pa' Watson, Roosevelt's chief of staff, which led Halifax to FDR himself. For the remainder of the war, Halifax developed a working relationship with the president that complemented FDR's ties to Churchill. Halifax also broke through to the country at large. Visiting isolationist Detroit in November 1941, he faced an angry crowd and a hail of eggs and tomatoes. Reacting calmly, his office later quoted him as saying 'how fortunate you Americans are, in Britain we only get one egg a week and we are glad of those'.[f] Halifax never uttered these words, but the remark saw his stock rise further. Thus by the time the United States entered the war, Halifax had established himself as an effective ambassador. As the representative of America's closest ally his popularity soared.

ABOVE Lord Halifax was featured on the cover of *Life* magazine shortly after he arrived in Washington in January 1941. He found the transition from aristocrat to ambassador challenging. After attending a baseball game, he was ridiculed by the American press for asking ignorant questions and leaving his hotdog uneaten on his seat.

Churchill and Roosevelt: Wartime Partners

Even before Halifax's appointment, Roosevelt had resolved to do more to help Britain. Lothian's outburst had been followed, in December 1940, by a private letter from Churchill, explaining the 'mortal danger' that Britain, no longer 'able to pay cash for shipping and other supplies', now faced.[8] Victorious in the November presidential election, Roosevelt proposed a policy known as 'Lend-Lease', allowing him to lend or lease war materials to Britain. Payment would be settled only after the war. FDR also forced the resignation of Joseph P. (Joe) Kennedy, the defeatist American ambassador in London, who opposed US help for Britain and proclaimed that democracy was 'finished in England' and might soon be in the United States.

American opinions were changing: 'One increasingly hears them talking now about when, not if, we get into the war', Halifax reported in April.[9] In the following months, Roosevelt edged closer to Britain. In August, he and Churchill met at Placentia Bay in Newfoundland. The resultant 'Atlantic Charter' laid down principles to shape the post-war world, including self-determination, free government and liberal economic policies. Nonetheless, it was only the Japanese attack on Pearl Harbor, on 7 December 1941, which brought America into the war. Hearing the news in the Residence, Lady Halifax asked for a bottle of champagne, 'explaining to their American butler, Maddams, that there had been a birth in the family'.[10]

Churchill now resolved to visit Washington. Would defeating Germany be Roosevelt's priority when only the Japanese had spilt American blood? On this and other issues, Churchill wanted to weigh in. At first, aware that many Americans remained resistant to the European theatre, Roosevelt was equivocal: 'he was not quite sure if your coming here might not be rather too strong medicine', Halifax reported.[11] The prime minister, however, would brook no dispute. He left for the United States aboard the battleship the *Duke of York*, on 12 December, arriving ten days later.

Churchill remained in North America for just over three weeks. Staying at the White House, he stuck close to FDR. As he reported to Clement Attlee, the leader of the Labour Party and deputy prime minister in Churchill's coalition government: 'We live here as a big family in the greatest intimacy and informality and I have formed the very highest regard and admiration for the President. His breadth of view, resolution and his loyalty to the common cause are beyond all praise.'[12]

These three weeks were important beyond measure. Close personal ties now coincided with shared national interests. Most importantly, defeating Germany became the agreed top priority. This was deeply reassuring to Churchill. He and Roosevelt also created the 'combined chiefs of staff', unifying the top bodies responsible for war policy in both countries, pooling raw materials and weaponry. It was an extraordinary melding of sovereignty, with each country yielding exclusive ability to conduct its own military planning.

At the end of Churchill's visit, Halifax's evaluation could not have been more positive: 'the immense usefulness of your personal contacts with F.D.R. will remain and grow, as the field of joint action widens', he wrote to Churchill. 'Altogether, the benefit is just not capable of being measured. I don't think you have ever done a better fortnight's work in value!'[13]

Halifax's prediction proved apt. As Britain and America fought side by side, a 'special relationship' was forged. This was both a union of national interests and a real friendship at the top. Roosevelt and Churchill used private envoys to nurture their relationship, above all Harry Hopkins, often circumventing the ambassadors in Washington and London. The two leaders also kept up a voluminous correspondence. By the time of Roosevelt's death, they had exchanged nearly two thousand written messages.

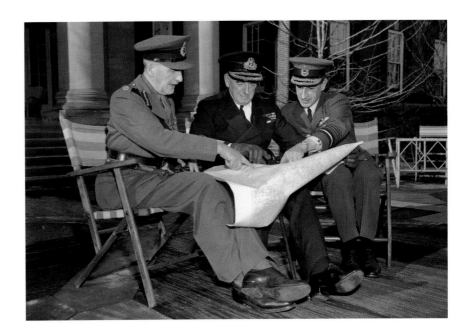

FACING PAGE Throughout the war the Residence played host to crucial meetings between the Allies. Here, members of the British Commonwealth missions meet in the Dining Room in 1943.
RIGHT The close military collaboration between the United Kingdom and the United States during the Second World War required the presence of senior British officers in Washington. Sir John Dill, at the left, was chief of the British Joint Staff Mission and hugely respected by the Americans. Here, on Christmas Day 1941, he studies a map with Chief of the Naval Staff Sir Dudley Pound and Air Chief Marshall Sir Charles Portal on the Lower Terrace.

Espionage at the Embassy and Beyond

With the war came unparalleled sharing of intelligence. Eventually codified by the 1946 UK-USA agreement, cooperation over signals intelligence became a crucial strand of the 'special relationship' that continues to this day. Yet in the beginning not all intelligence activities were entirely above board.

From 1940 onwards, British agents operated covertly against American targets, seeking to propel the United States into the war. The nerve centre for this effort was not the Embassy, but the British Security Coordination (BSC) office in New York, run by William Stephenson. Handpicked by Churchill, Stephenson became a legend in the espionage business. He not only planned operations on US soil, but at Camp X in Canada, he trained thousands of covert agents, who were dispatched across the world. Stephenson also proved a formative influence on the Office of Special Services (OSS), the precursor to the Central Intelligence Agency (CIA). Stephenson's agents included Roald Dahl, later the beloved children's author, then based at the Embassy as assistant air attaché. It was the perfect cover for the handsome Dahl, who wined, dined and slept his way through the Washington social scene, while feeding information back to Stephenson.

The Embassy, however, was not only a base for intelligence gathering but a target. 'I am sure we are being handicapped in negotiating with the United States by the way they always seem to know what we are going to do, before we have in fact told them', Ernest Bevin, the foreign secretary, reported to Attlee in December 1946. 'I am certain they have picked up a lot from the innumerable transatlantic telephone calls which have taken place between London and His Majesty's Embassy Washington.'[14]

Tensions at the Top

For all the strength of the Churchill-Roosevelt friendship, Britain and America did not always see eye-to-eye. As the wartime partnership evolved, tensions emerged of varying magnitudes.

Britain and America cooperated over the development of the atomic bomb, but bickered over who would take the lead. Although early on British research led the way, America soon roared ahead, leaving Britain far behind. Only in 1943, at the Quebec summit, did Roosevelt formally agree to a full collaborative partnership.

There was also tension over the timing of military campaigns. Throughout 1942, the American military were eager to open a second European front as early as 1943. Churchill, with an eye on British troops already committed elsewhere, and aware that the cross-Channel invasion, when it came, would have to be decisive, urged delay. More fundamentally, by mid-1943, Roosevelt was looking to the post-war situation. While he considered Churchill an indispensable ally, he had no intention of helping Britain retain its Empire. Roosevelt believed that the Soviet Union would be the dominant power in Europe after the war and was convinced that he could win over Stalin to forge a long-lasting US-Soviet friendship.

When Roosevelt, Stalin and Churchill met together for the first time, in Tehran in November 1943, there was a noticeable deterioration in Anglo-American relations. In his efforts to gain Stalin's confidence, Roosevelt regularly belittled Churchill. 'Winston got red and scowled, and the more he did so, the more Stalin smiled', Roosevelt later recalled.[15] Overriding Churchill's continued doubts, the conference confirmed operation 'Overlord', the invasion of France, as the absolute military priority, to be launched in the summer of 1944.

To Victory

D-Day fell on 6 June 1944. More British than American troops landed in Normandy that day, but from then on, America had more troops in combat than Britain. By December, Churchill admitted that 'it is not so easy as it used to be for me to get things done'.[16] Stalin, by contrast, was finding it easier and easier to get things done. When the Big Three met for the final time at Yalta, in February 1945, Soviet forces had already taken Poland and moved into the Balkans. Stalin promised that free elections would follow. On 6 March, however, a Soviet-dominated government was imposed in Romania and the elections promised for Poland came to nothing. Churchill now sought to reinforce his ties to Roosevelt. 'Our friendship is the rock on which I build for the future of the world so long as I am one of the builders', he wrote to the president in March: 'As I observed last time, when the war of the giants is over, the war of the pygmies will begin. There will be a torn, ragged and hungry world to help to its feet: and what will U.J. [Uncle Joe] or his successor say to the way we should both like to do it?'[17]

Roosevelt, however, did not live long enough to grapple with such issues. On 12 April, he suffered a brain haemorrhage and died. The succession of Roosevelt's vice president, Harry Truman, did nothing to hinder the course of the war. The German surrender came on 7 May and, after the dropping of atomic bombs on Hiroshima and Nagasaki, Japan followed suit on 14 August. These victories were due, in no small part, to the extraordinary closeness of the Anglo-American partnership. Within days, however, this relationship would come under severe strain.

ABOVE Although he became one
of Britain's most successful
ambassadors, Sir Oliver Franks
preferred the cerebral side of the job
to the social and once complained
that he had to spend far too
much time talking to people.
Here, he snatches a rare moment
of solitude with his family on
the Lower Terrace.

New Realities
Adjusting to the Post-War World, 1945–56

WITH THE WAR OVER, THERE WAS A GREAT DESIRE IN THE United States to bring the troops home and turn inwards. While America was booming, Britain was in dire financial straits, with an economy that had lost 25 percent of its pre-war value. Britain naturally looked to its wartime ally for help, but the Americans proved unreceptive. Old doubts crept in that Britain was trying to restore its Empire and pre-war economic dominance. British and American interests were no longer necessarily aligned. Anglo-American cooperation had reached dizzying heights during the war, but the cliff edge now beckoned.

Drifting Apart

A week after the Japanese surrender, Truman cut off Lend-Lease without warning or consultation. After Churchill's surprise loss at the polls in July, Clement Attlee was now prime minister of a Labour government. John Maynard Keynes, the leading economist of the era, warned Attlee's Cabinet that Britain faced a 'financial Dunkirk'. Mountains of debt and the need for reconstruction threatened to cripple the British economy, placing at risk plans for an extensive welfare state. Sent to Washington to negotiate aid, Keynes felt confident that he could secure a grant of $6 billion. But after desperately hard negotiations, all he could extract was a loan for $3.75 billion, repayable at 2 percent interest over fifty years.

This caused uproar in the House of Commons, where it was felt that the Americans were not fairly sharing the burdens of war. But the deal faced equally vicious attacks in Congress, who considered it far too generous. Why, asked one Congressman, should America support a Britain with 'too damned much Socialism at home and too much damned Imperialism abroad'?[1] With the loan in the balance, Churchill, although out of office, went to Washington to work his old magic. Wining and dining legislators at the Residence, he backed the loan, assuring them

that Attlee's ministers, his political enemies, were 'men of experience and understanding and were certainly not rash doctrinaire socialists, liable to go to extremes'.[2] Truman signed the bill into law on 15 July. As this battle raged, the United States also pulled back in the nuclear realm. The McMahon Act, signed into law in August 1946, forbade foreign nuclear collaboration, leading Britain to begin work on its own nuclear bomb.

Into this difficult climate stepped Lord Inverchapel, previously Sir Archibald Clark Kerr (and no relation to Philip Kerr, his predecessor but one), replacing Halifax as ambassador in May 1946. While an accomplished diplomat, Inverchapel never really took to Washington. His public-speaking ability and social skills, so important in that city, were limited: he avoided Washington society and loathed parties. More seriously, rather than steadfastly arguing the British position, he developed a reputation in London as too willing to accept the views being espoused by Washington. In late 1947, Bevin decided to replace him. Agreeing to leave in mid-1948, Inverchapel seemed only too happy:'I shall have by then rounded off about the toughest two years I have ever had. It will then be logical, proper and decent that I should be packed away in the museum amongst the mothballs whose fragrance becomes more and more alluring to me.'[3] Fortunately for Anglo-American relations, the inadequacies of Lord Inverchapel were eclipsed by the growing threat from the Soviet Union.

Uniting against Moscow

Initially the Americans had tried to hold on to Roosevelt's vision of Moscow as a partner, but as evidence mounted of Soviet subversion across Eastern Europe, the American mind began to shift. In March 1946, speaking in Fulton, Missouri, at Truman's invitation, Churchill warned of an 'iron curtain' descending across Europe and called for a 'special relationship between

the United States and the British Commonwealth'[4] to resist the spread of communism. Attlee's government, too, wanted to see a tougher line from Washington. While Attlee and Truman were not close personally, British and American interests were aligning once more.

Almost a year later, when Britain could no longer afford to fund the Greek government's efforts to resist a Soviet-backed insurgency, the United States agreed to pick up the tab. On 12 March, the president laid out the Truman Doctrine before Congress, whereby the United States would 'support free peoples who are resisting attempted subjugation by armed minorities or outside pressures'.[5] On 5 June 1947, George Marshall, the secretary of state, heralded the birth of what became known as the Marshall Plan, a massive programme of assistance for a hungry and vulnerable Europe. Congress proved resistant, but after the communists seized power in Czechoslovakia in February 1948, they approved $17 billion in aid to Europe. To London's relief, America was engaging in the world once more. The Cold War had begun.

The British government was delighted by the generosity of the Marshall Plan. Indeed, as an expression of gratitude, every year since 1954 around thirty of America's brightest graduate students have been awarded Marshall Scholarships to continue their studies at a British university. But, in the late 1940s, the Marshall Plan alone would not thwart Soviet ambitions. The next step was to persuade Washington to match money with military muscle. With Bevin in the vanguard, London appealed to the Americans for a commitment to the defence of Europe. It fell to the new British ambassador, Sir Oliver Franks, to bring this to fruition.

Arriving in Washington in early June 1948, Franks was not a typical ambassador. Austere with a phenomenal intellect, until the war Franks had spent much of his career in academia. While the Franks-era Embassy was not known for extravagant social occasions, Franks' powers of analysis and persuasion became legendary. He also proved particularly adept at cultivating important contacts, above all the secretary of state, Dean Acheson. Friends during the war, no sooner had Franks become ambassador than Acheson made him 'an unorthodox proposal',[6] the two would meet regularly and talk entirely off the record. Franks accepted and the relationship flourished. Combined with his talents, this gave Franks great influence in Washington.

In July 1948, Franks began talks in Washington with both the Americans and Europeans, aimed at creating a North Atlantic security pact. Through force of intellect, he assumed the mantle of unofficial moderator. Franks 'would summarise the discussion in a way which was so much clearer than anyone else', said one US diplomat, 'we were all entranced with the lucidity of the analysis'. While clearly representing his country, Franks 'did it in a way in which he became a US leader'.[7] By 24 December, a draft treaty had emerged. After subtle modifications to ensure Senate ratification, overseen informally by Franks and Acheson, the Treaty creating NATO was signed in Washington on 4 April 1949. The United States was now bound into the defence of Europe. It was a triumph for Anglo-American relations and, especially, for Oliver Franks.

Disagreements over Korea

If Britain and America saw eye-to-eye over the communist threat to Europe, elsewhere they began to differ. After North Korea invaded the South, on 25 June 1950, Truman secured a UN resolution authorising help for the South and called on Britain to join in sending troops. Advised by the chiefs of staff that Britain was already overstretched, Attlee hesitated. Franks now intervened. On 15 July, he wrote to the prime minister in his own hand, warning that the Americans would likely 'test the quality of the partnership by our attitude to the notion of a token ground force'.[8] Noting the strength of Franks' representation, Attlee overruled the military's doubts in the interests of 'Anglo-American solidarity'.[9] A British brigade was swiftly dispatched to Korea.

Britain was, in part, paying its dues for the 'special relationship', but the commitment also provided leverage over the Korean campaign. It did not, however, prevent Truman, at a press conference that November, from suggesting that, following military setbacks, the use of atomic weapons was under active consideration. This appalled Attlee, who immediately flew to Washington and extracted a private pledge that Truman would 'not consider the use of the bomb without consulting with the United Kingdom'.[10] Publicly the Americans would not go nearly so far, but useful ambiguities remained and the summit ended a potentially damaging split in the relationship.

Eden Rising: The Road to a Crisis

In the early 1950s, the principal actors in Anglo-American relations changed. In October 1951, the Conservatives defeated Labour and Churchill returned to power, bringing Anthony Eden as foreign secretary. A little over a year later, Dwight Eisenhower

(Ike) won the presidential election for the Republicans, appointing John Foster Dulles secretary of state. These years were not easy ones for the 'special relationship'. The confluence of Eden and Dulles, who shared personal animosity, contributed to this. But broader difficulties were now in play. While Britain struggled after a ruinously expensive war, America continued to rise and assume influence where Britain had once held sway. A process of adjustment was inevitable, but its course was neither smooth nor pleasant.

Following his return to power, Churchill was eager to visit Washington once more, believing he could restore the old wartime partnership. Many Americans feared that Britain was seeking more influence and concerns developed over a potential clash. In the event, Truman and Churchill proved the doubters wrong. The new president did not always tolerate Churchill waxing lyrical about the special relationship, but the two worked effectively together.

The 'Truman-Churchill understanding', which emerged from the meeting, stated that the use of US bases in Britain (where nuclear weapons were stationed) would be 'a matter for joint decision ... in the light of the circumstances prevailing at the time'.[11] This built on the 1950 Attlee-Truman understanding, offering Britain a useful form of words concerning US nuclear weapons on their soil. Churchill 'achieved a happy relation of confidence' with Truman, concluded Franks, and 'effectively dispelled the silly rumours circulating in Washington'.[12]

In January 1953, Sir Roger Makins succeeded Franks as ambassador. A career diplomat, Makins had already served in America twice and had married an American, Alice, the daughter of Dwight Davis, President Coolidge's secretary of state. This provided the perfect entrée into America's social scene. Unlike Franks, Makins entertained regularly and lavishly. 'Unusually tall and much less reserved than his compatriots he is a good con-

versationalist', noted his confidential State Department biography.[13] He was also well connected politically, having worked with Eisenhower during the Second World War.

That January, as Eisenhower prepared to assume the presidency, Churchill descended on Washington once more. It was not his happiest visit. After clashing with the incoming president over Egypt and the Middle East, Churchill told Makins that Eisenhower 'for all his qualities, did not show much political maturity'. At a lively dinner at the Residence with the outgoing Truman people, Churchill told them 'we would have been better off with the continuance in power of the men with whom we had been through so much together'.[14] Eisenhower, too, was not impressed. 'Winston is trying to relive the days of World War II', he wrote in his diary, suggesting he had 'developed an almost childlike faith that all of the answers are to be found merely in British-American partnership'.[15] Eisenhower, however, was not the only one to be sceptical of Churchill's vision for Anglo-American relations. As Makins worked hard to keep Britain and America together, he soon discovered that Eden, the foreign secretary and also his boss, had little patience with this approach.

In 1954, Anglo-American relations came close to crisis point over Indochina. The French, fighting the Chinese-backed communists in Vietnam, were on the verge of defeat. The Americans urged 'united action' to help the French, which Makins supported, but Eden refused. He saw Dulles' fears about a 'domino effect' in Indochina as far-fetched and felt intervention risked war with China. America, he believed, was simply trying to extend its sphere of influence. Without British support, Eisenhower refused to intervene and the French suffered a crippling defeat at Dien Bien Phu.

There followed a peace conference in Geneva in May. Dulles sulked throughout, while Eden complained furiously to his officials that 'all the Americans want to do is replace the French and run Indo-China themselves ... They want to run the world'.[16] Partnering with the Soviets, Eden delivered a settlement for Vietnam over American objections, winning him plaudits at home for standing up to Washington and keeping Britain out of war.

In April 1955, aged eighty, Churchill finally gave in to his failing health and stepped down as prime minister. He was succeeded by Eden, long his heir apparent. That October, Eden told his cabinet that Britain should no longer 'be restricted over-much by reluctance to act without full American concurrence and support'.[17] There was now little personal warmth between London and Washington and a sense of diverging interests. This helped precipitate the most serious crisis of post-war Anglo-American relations.

The Suez Debacle

On 26 July 1956, the president of Egypt, Gamal Abdel Nasser, nationalised the Suez Canal. Although Egypt had achieved independence in 1922, Britain maintained ownership of the canal, which remained an artery for Britain's oil supply. All this was now at risk, leaving Eden humiliated. In London there was a clear sense that Nasser had to go and Britain imposed immediate sanctions while preparing to use force. The problem, as Makins reported, was that the Eisenhower administration took a very different view: 'On the Suez business ... I would not say there was any support here for an attack on Egypt or for the use of force ... this is, of course, not meant in any sense as a criticism, but as an objective appraisal [of] which I would like you to be aware.'[18]

Eisenhower wanted Nasser gone but would not support overt military action, a throwback to the heyday of imperialism. Makins reported this as clearly as he could but London simply concluded he had 'gone native' and Eden discounted his advice.[19] Three years earlier, after all, the Americans had joined Britain in engineering a coup removing the democratically-elected prime minister, Mohammad Mossadegh, from power in Iran. On 11 October, Makins found himself recalled to London to become joint permanent secretary of the Treasury.

Eden now carefully excluded America. On 24 October, Britain, France and Israel made a secret pact. Israel would attack Egypt, after which Britain and France would restore peace, retaking the Suez Canal. Like the Americans, Makins had been kept in the dark. Returning to London, he discovered a 'kind of torpor', with no-one wanting to see him. 'I was astounded', Makins wrote later. 'It would never occur to me that we would go to war with Egypt without full American support, and I at once realised that this would end in disaster.'[20]

Makins' prediction held true. On 29 October, Israel attacked Egypt. And by 5 November, British and French paratroopers were on the ground. Taking advantage of this, on 4 November, the Soviets had sent tanks into Budapest, ending the Hungarian uprising. The Americans were beside themselves. Trying to reach Eden at Number 10, the president was connected to William Clark, the press secretary: 'Is that you, Anthony?' he asked angrily. 'Well, this is President Eisenhower, and I can only presume you have gone out of your mind.'[21]

The administration's response was swift. Britain's adventure had left her short on oil and currency reserves. On 6 November, the day of the US presidential election, the situation became critical and Britain approached America for aid. It had not occurred to anyone in London that America would refuse. But this is exactly what happened. Facing certain financial disaster, Britain ceased hostilities at midnight. Anglo-American relations had reached their nadir.

BELOW John Foster Dulles (left) and Anthony Eden appear to share a joke as Dulles arrives in London on 18 September 1954. The smiles are deceptive. Dulles and Eden were like two scorpions in a bottle, whose personal animosity hindered the conduct of UK-US relations.

STATE VISITS

The uniquely close nature of Anglo-American relations receives its most formal expression during the pomp and ceremony of a state visit. In June 1939, George VI became the first British monarch to make such a visit to the United States and his successor, Queen Elizabeth II, has followed closely in her father's footsteps. Her Majesty The Queen, as Princess Elizabeth, first visited America in 1951, as a guest of President Truman. Since then she has made no fewer than five state visits and numerous private trips.

In 1957, the newly-crowned Queen made her inaugural state visit, to the delight of President Eisenhower. Everywhere she went The Queen drew large crowds and the admiration of the American people. The centrepiece of her itinerary was a trip to Jamestown, Virginia, then celebrating its 350th anniversary as the first permanent settlement in the United States. Away from her formal duties, The Queen took in some American football, watching a game at Maryland University between the home team and North Carolina. Impressed by the size of the athletes she turned to her hosts and asked: 'Where do you get all those enormous players?'

In July 1976, The Queen returned to mark the US bicentennial. Once again, her visit proved a triumph. 'We may have lost this fair land in 1776', gushed 'The Wash', an internal Embassy newsletter, 'but last week on our behalf it was captured again ... This tremendous feat was accomplished by HM Queen Elizabeth II, using only her quiet serenity and charm that radiates from a 5'4" frame and a beautiful, disarming smile.' Following a state dinner at the White House, The Queen hosted a return banquet at the Residence the next evening. Here VIPs including Muhammad Ali, Elizabeth Taylor and Yehudi Menuhin dined alongside Washington's elite on saddle of lamb and frozen soufflé 'de l'Ambassade'. During her third state visit in 1983, The Queen paid public tribute to US support for Britain during the Falklands War the previous year. She visited President and Mrs Ronald Reagan at their ranch in California, before hosting a surprise party for the Reagans' thirty-first anniversary aboard the royal yacht *Britannia*. Returning in 1991, The Queen addressed Congress for the first time and travelled to Florida, where she presented General Norman Schwarzkopf, the US commander in the recently concluded Gulf War, with an honorary knighthood. Her most recent visit came in 2007 when she commemorated the 400th anniversary of the Jamestown Settlement and paid her respects at the newly opened World War II Memorial in Washington, while finding time to indulge her passion for horse racing at the Kentucky Derby.

TOP George VI and Queen Elizabeth in an open car as they leave the Residence in Washington on 13 June 1939.

BOTTOM Visiting the United States in 1951, Queen Elizabeth II, then Princess Elizabeth, is accompanied by her host, President Truman. Princess Elizabeth stayed not at the Residence but at the US government's official guest house, Blair House, opposite the White House. She followed this precedent for all subsequent state visits to Washington.

RIGHT Making her first state
visit to the United States in 1957,
The Queen greets President
Eisenhower as he arrives
at the Residence for dinner
on 19 October. State visits
traditionally feature a dinner at
the White House for the monarch
followed by a 'return dinner' at
the Residence for the president,
hosted by The Queen.

FACING PAGE The Queen dances with President Gerald Ford at the White House during her second state visit, to mark the American bicentennial, in July 1976. Not everyone was amused by the Marine band's decision to strike up 'The Lady is a Tramp' shortly after she took to the dance floor.

ABOVE (CLOCKWISE FROM TOP, LEFT) Actress Elizabeth Taylor meets The Queen and President Gerald Ford at the Residence in 1976; President George H. W. Bush and Mrs Barbara Bush pose with The Queen and The Duke of Edinburgh against the elegant backdrop of the Ambassador's Study prior to a dinner hosted by The Queen at the Residence on 16 May 1991; The Queen and The Duke of Edinburgh arrive under the Portico for a garden party celebrating her state visit to the United States on 7 May 2007.

Restoring the Relationship
From Ike to JFK, 1956–63

AS MAKINS PUT IT, THE SUEZ AFFAIR MARKED 'THE END OF an era' in Anglo-American relations. But all was not necessarily lost. Prior to Suez, he argued, the administration had been 'willing to deal with us on a special and favourable basis'. But Britain had not always reciprocated. 'At all times during my mission', concluded Makins, 'the key to Anglo-American relations lay in London and not in Washington.'[1] Could London now pick up the pieces?

Picking up the Pieces
On the ground, this task fell to Britain's new man in Washington, Sir Harold Caccia. A Foreign Office heavyweight, Caccia had long enjoyed Eden's favour and had confidently expected to take the helm as permanent undersecretary, the organisation's professional head. However, largely at Makins' urging, Eden agreed that Caccia should succeed him. Sir Harold was not amused. In one of those cricketing analogies so dear to British aficionados of the sport, he complained that: 'Nancy and I have all that sensation of being asked to open an innings at Lords, when we really are not bats at all.'[2]

At first, Eisenhower (Ike) too was less than enthusiastic, telling Dulles he was 'sorry Makins is going'. Caccia, said Dulles, was 'smart though not same calibre as Makins'.[3] His confidential State Department biography was more positive. '[W]ell known to American officials', Caccia was said to possess an 'exceptionally fine agile mind and great professional skill ... His manner is affable and charming and he displays little of the reserve or aloofness characteristic of some British diplomats.'[4]

Arriving in Washington on 7 November 1956, Caccia's early weeks as ambassador were exceptionally fraught. Following Suez, large parts of the American administration were virtually not speaking to their British contacts. 'I see no reason for despondency', Caccia wrote, nonetheless, in January: 'the new era is one of more strictly business relationships, with much sentiment cut out and our special position temporarily, at least, impaired, but not totally dissipated'.[5]

What was really needed was a change of heads at the top. The administration had lost faith in Eden and a collective sigh of relief greeted his resignation on 9 January 1957. Like Churchill, Eden's successor, Harold Macmillan, had a natural affinity for America (as well as an American mother). He knew and liked Eisenhower, having worked with him during the war, and was determined to restore ties.

Eisenhower, delighted by Macmillan's promotion, offered to meet the new prime minister in Bermuda, in March. The resulting summit was friendly, but not without plain speaking: 'I made it clear that the British people felt "let down" by America', Macmillan recorded in his diary. '... The President took this up rather sharply in his reply, which was very gracious and very fair.'[6] The discussions cleared the air and the personal breach was healed.

At Bermuda, Eisenhower took a significant step towards restoring nuclear cooperation. American 'Thor' missiles would be based in Britain and launched only with agreement from both countries. In October 1957, Eisenhower proposed an end to the McMahon Act, which had cut Britain out of the nuclear loop back in 1946. Having exploded its own H-bomb that May, Britain now had technical expertise to offer. More importantly, the recent Soviet launch of Sputnik, the world's first satellite, had shocked Washington and reinforced a desire to draw close to Britain. In July 1958, the US-UK Mutual Defence Agreement was signed, restoring full nuclear cooperation. In 1960, Eisenhower agreed to make Skybolt, an air-launched missile that carried nuclear warheads, available to Britain, whose own missile system, Blue Streak, was proving an expensive flop. In return, the United States gained a base for its submarines at Holy Loch in Scotland.

These were bilateral agreements of major importance, which continue to govern UK-US nuclear cooperation to this day. Thanks to the confluence of close personal ties and a renewed sense of threat from the Soviet Union, the 'special relationship' had been restored.

JACK AND DAVID

Discussing a replacement for Harold Caccia at Key West, President Kennedy argued strongly for his great friend Sir David Ormsby Gore, who was also a minister in Macmillan's government. Macmillan was happy to oblige: 'You see, the President had three lives', he explained: 'he had his smart life, dancing with people not in the political world at all, smart people, till four in the morning; then he had his highbrow life ... and then he had his political life. And David belonged to all three.'[a]

William David Ormsby Gore came from the storied ranks of British society. His father was the 4th Baron Harlech and his great-grandfather was the prime minister Lord Salisbury.

A Conservative member of Parliament (MP) from 1950, Ormsby Gore rose to be minister of state under Macmillan. While not a scholar, he was a man of great intelligence with a shrewd understanding of politics. Yet he remained 'conscious that he was an aristocrat', said his private secretary, Christopher Everett. 'He was unfailingly kind to those who worked for him, but he was clear that there was a difference and of course the Kennedys took the same view, and they reinforced each other.'[b]

Ormsby Gore first met Kennedy in 1938 in London, when the latter's father, Joe Kennedy, was ambassador to the Court of St James. In 1944, Kathleen 'Kick' Kennedy, the future president's sister, married William Cavendish, the dashing son of the 10th Duke of Devonshire and heir to the magnificent Chatsworth House estate. Ormsby Gore was Cavendish's cousin and was now drawn closer into the Kennedy orbit. Kick's marriage ended tragically after only four months when her husband was killed in action in Belgium, but the family ties endured. By the time Kennedy became president, his friendship with Ormsby Gore was assured.

Unless the president was abroad, the Ormsby Gores would regularly spend time at the weekends with the Kennedys. 'It was very much of a holiday weekend for the President', the ambassador reported after one such jaunt, 'and we spent most of the time swimming and boating.'[c] On other occasions, Ormsby Gore hosted 'reading evenings' in the Residence, a confidential book club which members of the Kennedy clan would attend.

So close were Ormsby Gore and Kennedy that the president felt confident sharing his intimate thoughts and seeking advice. Balancing his role as friend and ambassador, Ormsby Gore passed back nuggets of insight to London, ensuring that Macmillan always knew what Kennedy was thinking. But Ormsby Gore's influence on Kennedy was subtle. As one US official put it, 'he had a knack of getting in the British views at the early stages so we took them into account *before* we came to a conclusion'.[d] Above all, it was known in Washington that the British ambassador had the president's ear. And this, in a town that prized access to power, was an asset no other country could match.

PAGE 89 Jacqueline Kennedy and Sir David and Lady Ormsby Gore arrive at the National Theatre in Washington in June 1962. The strength of the personal friendship between the Embassy and the White House during the Kennedy era has not been matched before or since.

ABOVE Given their personal ties, President Kennedy and Ormsby Gore were expected to work well together. More surprising was the genuine friendship that grew up between the British prime minister, Harold Macmillan, and the far younger Kennedy. Here, the president, the first lady, Macmillan and the Ormsby Gores take a stroll in the White House grounds in April 1962.

Macmillan and Kennedy: An Unlikely Bond

On 2 November 1960, Caccia told Macmillan that he now expected John F. Kennedy (known colloquially as 'JFK' and to friends and family as Jack) to succeed Eisenhower in the imminent presidential election. This prediction proved spot on. The prime minister was very worried. He had nurtured a friendship with Eisenhower for over 'twenty years of war and peace' and could therefore 'appeal to memories. With this new and comparatively young President', he told Alec Douglas Home, the foreign secretary, 'we have nothing of the kind to draw on'.[7]

To remedy this, Macmillan looked for an early meeting. Caccia urged caution, preferring to prepare the ground. But Macmillan would have none of it. When the president suggested a meeting in Key West, Florida, in March 1961, Macmillan jumped at the chance.

This first meeting proved a modest success, but the relationship deepened after Kennedy visited London that June. This was a very difficult time for the president. The botched US-backed attempt to invade Cuba and depose Fidel Castro ('The Bay of Pigs') that April had drained his authority. He came to London hot on the heels of a summit with Khrushchev in Vienna, during which the Soviet premier had sought to bully and browbeat the new president. Sensing Kennedy's mood, and his exhaustion, Macmillan pounced: 'Let's not have a meeting – the Foreign Office and all that', he said. 'Why not have a peaceful drink and chat by ourselves?'[8] Kennedy was delighted to accept and, over whisky and sandwiches, they spoke frankly about his encounter with Khrushchev. 'He was kind, intelligent, and very friendly', Macmillan noted, '... K looks like being a good friend to me.'[9]

In July 1961, the outgoing Harold Caccia had submitted a lukewarm evaluation of Kennedy's first six months, concluding that 'British interests have not yet suffered serious harm'.[14] By year's end, with Ormsby Gore facilitating, the picture was decidedly rosier. Meeting in Bermuda that December, Kennedy and Macmillan stayed under the same roof: 'other than breakfast we had every meal together', recalled Ormsby Gore, who considered this 'the first occasion on which they really sized each other up and decided that they very much liked each other's company'.[15]

By the end of 1961, a real bond existed between the president and prime minister. But it was not all plain sailing. In August 1962, Kennedy agreed to sell Hawk missiles to Israel, ignoring a long-standing commitment to consult first with Britain. 'I cannot believe that you were party to this disgraceful piece of treachery', Macmillan wrote to Kennedy, 'Nor do I see how you and I are to conduct the great affairs of the world on this basis.'[16] Although these words stung, Kennedy allowed the storm to blow over, blaming his own bureaucracy. For both men, far greater challenges lay ahead.

The Cuban missile crisis

On Sunday 21 October 1962, Ormsby Gore became the first foreign diplomat to see photographic evidence of Soviet nuclear missiles in Cuba. Presenting this to the ambassador personally, Kennedy explained that there were four possible responses – an air strike on Cuba, an invasion, a naval blockade or acceptance of the missiles – and asked Ormsby Gore what he would do. Ormsby Gore chose the blockade, which Kennedy found useful confirmation of a decision he had already made. The next day a so-called 'quarantine' went into effect, blocking all shipping to Cuba.

As the crisis terrified the world, the Embassy was not immune: the mood in Washington 'was frightening', said Ormsby Gore. 'We dusted off the Embassy evacuation orders.'[17] Months earlier, Kennedy had confided his fear that the American people would be willing to go to the brink of nuclear war without even talking to Moscow: 'if he cared to tell the people that it was useless to negotiate', Kennedy told Ormsby Gore, 'they would probably agree with him.'[18] Now, however, the president sought to avoid exactly this scenario.

Kennedy was in touch with Macmillan regularly throughout, but as Ormsby Gore later commented: 'I can't honestly think of anything said from London that changed the US action – it was chiefly reassurance to JFK.'[19] The ambassador himself was more influential. Acting, in effect, as a personal advisor to the president, he persuaded Kennedy to draw the line for the 'quarantine' closer to Cuba than originally planned and to publish some intelligence photos to build public support. But the main decisions were Kennedy's alone. The quarantine, which succeeded in stopping Soviet ships peacefully, was his call as was a secret reciprocal offer to the Soviets to withdraw outdated US missiles from Turkey. When the Soviets backed down, on Sunday 28 October, and agreed to remove their missiles from Cuba, Macmillan was delighted. Kennedy never told him about the secret deal over Turkey.

Securing Britain's Nuclear Future

Just days after the Cuban crisis, the special relationship faced its own crisis. This too concerned nuclear weapons, but the arsenals of friends not enemies. At issue was Skybolt, the system Eisenhower had promised to Macmillan in 1960, but which the US defence secretary, Robert McNamara, now wanted to cancel on grounds of cost and poor performance. America would still have its Polaris submarine-launched missile system but Britain would be left with no way to deliver its nuclear warheads.

Ormsby Gore told McNamara that cancellation would be 'political dynamite',[20] but no action followed. Some in the administration now saw a chance to put an end to Britain's independent nuclear deterrent. These so-called 'Europeanists' wanted to force Britain to adjust to a lesser position in the world and integrate further with Europe. While Macmillan was determined that Britain would join the European Economic Community (EEC), he did not believe this should come at the expense of ties with the United States and had pledged to retain Britain's nuclear capacity.

Meeting Kennedy at Nassau in late December, Macmillan lobbied exceptionally hard. Ormsby Gore had already made the president aware of the importance of the issue. This the prime minister now reinforced with a powerful oration, warning that his political survival was at stake. Several compromises were proposed, but Macmillan held out until Kennedy offered Polaris. While committed to a NATO force, the missiles would remain British and could be used independently, should London judge 'that supreme national interests are at stake'.[21]

'I enjoyed our talks in the Bahamas', Macmillan wrote to Kennedy. 'Although rather strenuous, I think they were rewarding.'[22] Here was some classic British understatement. Although the ambiguity over the NATO commitment was not well received at home, the Nassau agreement proved Macmillan's masterstroke. Britain's nuclear deterrent had been guaranteed. So much of this had been made possible by the strength of his relationship with Kennedy. The lingering irony was that this triumph, pulling Britain closer to America, reinforced European opposition to Britain's membership of the EEC. In January 1963, de Gaulle formally vetoed Britain's application, leaving Macmillan's plans in ruins.

In 1963, UK-US relations began to wane as Macmillan's domestic position deteriorated. In June, his secretary of state for war, John Profumo, was forced to resign after his affair with a call girl, Christine Keeler, was exposed. Keeler, it emerged, was also involved with the Soviet defence attaché in London. Even as his government was rocked by this potential threat to national security, Macmillan kept his eye on the world stage. Since the late 1950s, Ormsby Gore had taken a great interest in nuclear arms control and worked, almost alone, to cultivate a similar interest in Kennedy. After repeated exhortations, the president now lent support to efforts to negotiate a nuclear test ban treaty with the Soviets. With the British in the driving seat, a partial ban was signed in August. Macmillan left office in October 1963, making this their last major act together.

When, in the early afternoon of 22 November 1963, news that President Kennedy had been shot reached the Residence, the mood was raw and emotional. Ormsby Gore was not prone to such displays, but for much of that afternoon he sat in the Morning Room with his wife Sissie, quietly weeping as officials attended him.'Kennedy's assassination hit the Embassy like a family bereavement because we all knew, even those not working closely with the ambassador, we all knew what a dreadful personal, quite apart from political, disaster it was for the Ormsby Gores.'[23]

In the days that followed, Ormsby Gore was in and out of the White House, but the ground was already shifting. Kennedy's death proved a turning point for his mission. Ormsby Gore had lost not only a close friend, but his most important ally in Washington.

LEFT Combining several icons of Anglo-American relations, President Kennedy, with David Ormsby Gore to his right, and Randolph Churchill representing his father to his left, proclaims Winston Churchill an honorary citizen of the United States during a ceremony at the White House on 10 April 1963.

THE NEW CHANCERY

The Second World War saw the Embassy expand far beyond anything ever envisaged by Lutyens. In the 1940s and early 1950s, four new plots of land had been acquired (shown as plots 37 and 43–45 on the map on page 36) adjacent to Lutyens' Embassy to the north. During the war, this new, enlarged site was plagued by temporary buildings, while other staff were dispersed to offices around the city. The case for constructing a permanent Chancery on the new land to the north now became inescapable.

British diplomatic buildings were then routinely designed by an in-house team of architects at the Ministry of Works led by Eric Bedford. His team submitted several designs, but the Royal Fine Art Commission, charged with vetting the proposals, was deeply unimpressed. Branding the designs 'completely undistinguished', the Commission suggested bringing in an outside architect 'to produce something really first class'.[a] But the Ministry of Works resisted, and Bedford's team happily tweaked their design.

The supreme irony is that the new Chancery utilised steel and concrete, the materials that Lutyens abhorred. A boxy office building of little character was erected, with a large interior courtyard. A rotunda was attached on the north side of the building. Despite the designs finding few admirers on either side of the Atlantic, the Embassy was in desperate need of more space and so the proposals moved forward regardless. In 1957, The Queen laid the cornerstone and the building opened in September 1960.

ABOVE, LEFT TO RIGHT
Queen Elizabeth II helps lay the cornerstone for the new Chancery building, on 19 October 1957, with the ambassador, Sir Harold Caccia, to her right. There emerged, in 1960, a building that has been unloved since birth and which several ambassadors have sought, unsuccessfully, to have torn down.

ABOVE At a meeting at the White House on 8 February 1968, Harold Wilson, the British prime minister, receives the famous 'Johnson treatment', as the president's wild gesticulations and unvarnished commentary rain down upon him. Johnson was renowned for his willingness to invade others' personal space and Wilson, whom Johnson never liked, appears appropriately uncomfortable.

A Difficult Period
LBJ and Wilson, Nixon and Heath, 1963–76

ORMSBY GORE KNEW THAT HIS RELATIONSHIP WITH THE new president, Lyndon B. Johnson (LBJ), 'was never going to be the same'.[1] Sure enough, when the British Cabinet directed Ormsby Gore to seek a meeting with the president, Johnson resisted. 'I'm not going to start seeing all these Ambassadors', he told McGeorge Bundy, his national security advisor. 'I don't care how many Cabinets are involved!'[2] Ormsby Gore continued to see Kennedy's advisors, retained by Johnson, often on the Residence's tennis court. However, they were no longer talking to someone who had the ear of their president and his influence waned.

A Relationship Diminished:
The Johnson and Wilson Years

Johnson's hostility rested not only on Ormsby Gore's close relationship with Kennedy, whose shadow the new president wanted to escape, but also on his inexperience in foreign policy. This born-and-bred Texan had neither a feel for Anglo-American relations nor an instinctive affinity with Britain. There was little warmth during the brief prime ministership of Alec Douglas Home and the election of Labour's Harold Wilson, in October 1964, offered no improvement. Visiting Washington that December, Wilson was unable to befriend LBJ. He was simply 'too ordinary', said one aide, and 'Johnson took an almost instant dislike to him'.[3] For much of the visit, the president complained privately that seeing Wilson was a waste of time. 'There is just no way in the world', responded Bundy in some desperation, 'that a President of the United States can avoid reasonably regular visits from the Prime Minister of Great Britain.'[4]

Nor did the appointment of a new ambassador, Sir Patrick Dean, in April 1965, ameliorate the situation. Dean was a shy man and not an obvious soulmate for the brash Johnson. When he presented his credentials, Johnson berated him, warning that he did not expect his allies to 'stab him in the back or slap him in the face'. The notoriously physical Johnson then 'slapped his own face quite vigorously'.[5] Weighing all this, Dean warned against confronting Johnson, who would only interpret this as betrayal: 'uncomfortable and infuriating though the position must be for British Ministers, we do stand to gain quite a lot by putting up, so far as we possibly can, with the President and his pretty outrageous behaviour'.[6]

The Johnson years were a troubled period for Anglo-American relations. A clash of personalities now overlay diverging national interests. Britain and America no longer shared the same perspective on their relative roles in the world and events only drove them further apart.

Vietnam proved a lingering sore. As LBJ led the United States deeper into the conflict, he appealed for British military support. Wilson provided moral backing but, under great pressure from his left wing, refused to send even a token force. Worse, Wilson tried to act as mediator in the dispute and infuriated Johnson by criticising US actions (such as the bombing raids on North Vietnam in February 1965) and suggesting immediate visits to Washington. There was a clear echo of Attlee's visit to Truman in 1950, pulling a supposedly out-of-control president back into line. Johnson was not impressed: 'we got enough pollution around here already', he complained, 'without Harold coming over with his fly open and his pecker hanging out, peeing all over me'.[7]

Johnson found Wilson's conduct particularly galling given the scale of American financial support for Britain, aimed at propping up an overvalued pound. Fearing that if sterling succumbed, the dollar would be next, and desperate for Britain to retain its military presence east of Suez, the United States helped London stave off devaluation. American support would continue, Wilson told the Cabinet in late 1965, so long as 'we stood firm on our present position in the Far East'.[8]

Two years later, Britain's financial position became unsustainable. On 17 November 1967, Dean informed Johnson that sterling would be devalued. Wilson's government now had Britain's commitments east of Suez in its sights. In January 1968, Dean tried to hold the line, arguing that if Britain abandoned 'the non-European world in terms of our defence and commitment, we shall have crossed a watershed in our ability to influence world affairs and above all ... Anglo-American relations'.[9] But it was to no avail. On 16 January, the government announced that virtually all forces in the Middle East and East Asia would be withdrawn by the end of 1971. Furious, Johnson told Wilson that he could no

THE BEATLES AT THE EMBASSY

In the midst of crises and the serious business of diplomacy, the Residence has also seen its lighter moments. On 11 February 1964, the Beatles played their first live stage show in America, at the Washington Coliseum. In the evening they visited the Residence for a 'champagne party and masked charity ball' being held in their honour. This was unusual. The sharply dressed diplomats and other notables were a world apart from the company the band customarily kept and this was not the sort of function they often attended.

The ambassador, Sir David Ormsby Gore, did his best to bridge the two worlds, laughing gamely when Ringo looked him up and down and asked, 'So, what do you do?' The other guests, who kept trying to touch the band, proved more of a problem. One slightly drunk woman draped herself around Paul, and insisted he tell her his name. 'Roger. Roger McClusky the Fifth', he replied swiftly. The final straw came when Ringo felt a sharp pull on his hair. He spun round and discovered that a crazed fan had hacked off a lock using her nail scissors. 'This lot here are terrifying', he shouted, 'much worse than the kids.'[a] In time the Beatles would conquer America, but that night they beat a hasty retreat.

ABOVE The Beatles appear relaxed during their brief visit to the Residence on 11 February 1964 as the ambassador (top right) looks on. In fact, they found the whole experience incredibly awkward.

longer consider Britain 'a valuable ally in any strategic theatre'.[10] Anglo-American relations plunged to a low not seen since Suez.

Mired in Vietnam, Johnson chose not to stand in the 1968 presidential election and Richard Nixon, a Republican, emerged the victor. This was not the outcome Wilson had expected. Prior to the election, the British government had announced that John Freeman, a former Labour MP turned editor of the *New Statesman*, would succeed Dean as ambassador in 1969. Freeman, who had openly criticised Nixon as 'a man of no principle whatsoever except a willingness to sacrifice everything in the cause of Dick Nixon',[11] was an overtly political choice designed to boost Wilson's links to the Democratic White House. Now he would have to find a way to deal with Nixon or risk humiliation.

The new president initially told aides he would have nothing to do with Freeman. When Nixon visited London in February 1969, recalled Henry Kissinger, the president's advance man 'asked for Freeman to be excluded from the 10 Downing Street dinner, but the British, to their great credit, refused'.[12] His protest made, Nixon buried the hatchet. 'Some say there's a new Nixon', he declared during his dinner toast. 'And they wonder if there's a new Freeman. I would like to think that's all behind us. After all, he's the new diplomat and I'm the new statesman.'[13] Later on, felt Kissinger, Freeman became perhaps Nixon's favourite foreign ambassador.

None too fond of Nixon, Wilson delayed visiting Washington until January 1970. He and the president put on a united front, but neither really trusted the other. Wilson's withdrawal east of Suez stuck in the American mind. The continuing Vietnam War remained a sore point for Wilson. In May, his foreign secretary, Michael Stewart, met Nixon and lectured him on foreign policy. This, Kissinger told Freeman, particularly Stewart's 'patronising' manner, 'left the President feeling irritated and somewhat baffled'.[14] It was a fitting end to the Nixon-Wilson era.

Heath and Nixon: From Great Promise to Great Despair

The Conservative victory in the general election of June 1970 heralded great hope for Anglo-American relations. Nixon was thrilled by Edward Heath's emergence as prime minster, telling Freeman that he expected 'a real meeting of minds'. Following Heath's strong backing over Vietnam and his decision to commit 4,500 troops east of Suez, relations between Britain and the United States were now 'extremely good', judged Freeman: Nixon 'regarded Britain as his closest and most trusted ally'. [15]

In February 1971, George Rowland Stanley Baring, the 3rd Earl of Cromer, replaced Freeman as ambassador. A Tory grandee, Cromer had been governor of the Bank of England, but most importantly was close to Heath, helping out during the election campaign by writing newspaper articles critical of Wilson. As Lord Powell, Cromer's private secretary, put it: Heath 'wanted his own man, somebody he could trust, in Washington'.[16]

The relationship, however, soon soured. Neither Heath nor Nixon were warm, charming individuals and they found social interaction difficult. They never established a rapport. Beyond this, problems arose from the secretive manner in which Nixon and Kissinger operated, often excluding their own State Department, not to mention the British. In August 1971, Nixon took the United States off the gold standard, threatening the bedrock of the international financial system. Heath was not consulted. 'The Americans no longer consider it necessary to consult with the UK as an imperial or world power', warned Cromer. 'They consult us when it is useful to them and not because they have to.'[17]

The most serious problem, however, came over Europe where perceived national interests were again diverging. Heath's overriding ambition was to see Britain join the EEC, which he felt required downgrading UK-US relations: 'it was almost inevitable that we should ruffle the feathers of the United States in the course of our negotiations for entering Europe', warned Freeman in 1970.[18] Pursuing this goal, Heath spoke of a 'natural' rather than a 'special' relationship and warned Nixon that Britain could not be 'America's Trojan Horse in Europe'.[19] By 1972, the Americans noted 'a growing conviction in London that the Anglo-American link becomes less unique and exclusive with each passing year'.[20]

In January 1973, Britain finally joined the EEC. But still Nixon held out hope. That February, Heath visited Washington. 'We've got to have a friend in Europe', Nixon told Kissinger privately, 'and he's the only solid partner we've got.'[21] But it was not to be. In April, Kissinger launched an initiative called the 'Year of Europe'. He intended Britain and America to take the lead in strengthening the Atlantic alliance. To Kissinger's fury, Heath refused, insisting that Britain contribute to a unified European response. It amounted to a full-throated rejection of the special relationship: 'For the sake of an abstract doctrine of European unity,' bemoaned Kissinger, 'something which had been nurtured for a generation was being given up.'[22]

The Arab-Israeli war that October caused further friction. The United States urged support for Israel, fearing Soviet encroachment in the Middle East. Britain, however, like other Europeans, remained reliant on Arab oil, which – thanks to OPEC – now doubled and quadrupled in price. London objected to an American-proposed UN resolution tilted against the Arabs and made clear that British bases could not be used to resupply Israel. Most seriously, on 25 October, after the Soviets suggested deploying troops to the region, the United States raised the alert status of its forces worldwide to DEFCON III. Cromer, alone amongst foreign ambassadors, was given early warning. But Britain was informed, not consulted. The fact that the United States had single-handedly risked conflict with the Soviets rankled in London.

As relations between the capitals deteriorated, the Embassy sought to pick up the slack. This was not completely successful. Although Nixon considered Cromer a 'very good, solid guy', Kissinger felt that he 'was not a type who could, through his human qualities, make up for' the deficiencies in the relationship.[23] The differences over issues were now too pronounced. Seeing Cromer in November, Kissinger expressed his sadness that 'the special relationship was collapsing'. He felt that Britain's entry into Europe 'should have raised Europe to the level of Britain. Instead it had reduced Britain to the level of Europe'.[24]

The Ford Interlude

In 1974, the principal actors on the Anglo-American stage changed again. In early March, Heath was defeated at the polls and Harold Wilson returned to Number 10. Before leaving office Heath had chosen Sir Peter Ramsbotham, a career diplomat, to be the next ambassador. Wilson confirmed the choice and, with the Watergate scandal in full flow, left Ramsbotham to handle Britain's relationship with the embattled White House. Five months later, Nixon resigned rather than face impeachment and Gerald Ford became president.

These changes marked an improvement, but not a dramatic shift, in Anglo-American relations. Kissinger, retained by Ford, was delighted to see the back of Heath, whom he considered the most anti-American prime minister in living memory. Britain's chronic economic weakness was now undermining its value as America's ally. In 1976, shortly after Callaghan replaced Wilson as prime minister, matters came to a head.

On 4 June 1976, facing yet another run on the pound, the British government approached Washington for support. This time the US administration refused, insisting Britain negotiate a loan with the IMF conditional on painful public expenditure cuts. Although tremendously difficult medicine for a Labour government to swallow, Callaghan eventually accepted the deal after Ford agreed to ease the terms somewhat. It proved a lifeline, but also a humiliation. Britain's standing in the world now reached a new low.

Special Relationships
Towards the Thatcher Decade, 1976–90

Carter, Callaghan and a Mild Improvement

The presidency of Jimmy Carter saw a further improvement in the tone of Anglo-American relations, overseen by a new ambassador. Yet the transition from Sir Peter Ramsbotham, a distinguished career diplomat, to Peter Jay, a distinguished journalist, proved awkward. The foreign secretary, David Owen, had insisted on recalling the experienced Ramsbotham in favour of someone more in tune with his own ideas. This proved hugely controversial, not least because Jay was Callaghan's son-in-law. Ramsbotham took the news badly. Asked, in April 1977, to leave by the end of May, he exploded. This, Ramsbotham felt, would be 'to treat him as one would barely treat a junior employee suspected of some kind of misdemeanour' noted an internal memo. 'He refused to be slung out on his ear.'[1] Furthermore, Ramsbotham had already built close ties to the new administration: 'if I had my druthers', Carter told him, 'you would not be leaving'.[2] Owen, however, was unmovable. And Callaghan acquiesced.

Carter understood how close Jay was to the prime minister, and he responded well to both of them. 'I was amazed how quickly Callaghan succeeded in establishing himself as Carter's favourite, writing him friendly little notes, calling, talking like a genial older uncle', commented Zbigniew Brzezinski, the national security advisor.[3] The two leaders became friends and, governing from the left, political allies. In February 1978, Jay told Callaghan that Carter had 'expressed great delight at what he described as your political resurgence'.[4] On another occasion, Carter openly admired Callaghan's suit, particularly the thousands of tiny 'J.C.' initials that made up its stripes. Callaghan promptly sent over the material and Carter had his own made.

While Carter and Callaghan were wearing the same clothes, British and American interests were not always so well-matched. Both countries faced huge economic challenges at home, which consumed much of their attention. When Callaghan suggested, in February 1978, united action to improve the world economy,

he found little enthusiasm in Washington. Carter, meanwhile, focused intently on bringing peace to the Middle East, with little role for the UK. There were no crises for Anglo-American relations during these years, but neither were there any great triumphs. After recent turbulence some harmony had returned, but as a classified CIA report put it, the special relationship had 'lost much of its meaning'.[5]

Enter Mrs Thatcher

In May 1979, Margaret Thatcher defeated Callaghan at the polls. Carter, who had met Thatcher previously, was less than thrilled. Politically they were miles apart and the new prime minister's assertive style grated. 'I think it will take patience to deal with Thatcher's hard-driving nature and tendency to hector', warned Brzezinski.[6]

The relationship between Carter and Thatcher was never warm, but always proper. Both believed in close Anglo-American relations, particularly Thatcher. After the onset of the Iran hostage crisis, in November 1979, British officials, concerned with commercial interests in the Middle East, argued for a cautious response. Thatcher chose a different course. 'At times like this you are entitled to look to your friends for support', she proclaimed while visiting Washington that December. 'We are your friends ... And we shall support you.'[7] Before the year was out, events pulled Britain and America closer together. When the Soviet Union invaded Afghanistan on Christmas Day 1979, Carter was shocked. He had dedicated his presidency to reducing tensions with the Soviets. All this now seemed for naught. Thatcher, while deeply disturbed, was not shocked. For years she had been warning of Soviet aggression and she felt vindicated. As Carter took a far tougher line with Moscow, she supported him to the hilt, but privately harboured doubts about his leadership. Only with the election of Ronald Reagan as president, in November 1980, did she find the partner she had been waiting for.

'NICKO' HENDERSON

After Thatcher became prime minister, a change in ambassadors was inevitable. Thatcher first offered the post to Edward Heath, largely because she did not want him anywhere else in her government. Given Heath's chequered history with the United States, it was a strange offer: 'who ever heard of a former Prime Minister running an Embassy?', he exclaimed and promptly rejected it.[a]

The Thatcher government now turned to Sir Nicholas 'Nicko' Henderson, just retired as ambassador in Paris. A deeply respected diplomat, Henderson had caught Thatcher's eye following the leak of his farewell dispatch deploring Britain's economic performance. She agreed with his views and admired his plain speaking. Henderson was sent to Washington in July 1979.

The appointment proved an inspired one. 'Coming out of retirement Henderson was quite happy to take well-judged risks', said Charles Anson, one of his press secretaries. 'And his efforts paid off in spades, both diplomatically and in the media. He was simply brilliant.'[b] With a razor-sharp mind, but famously unkempt appearance, Barbara Bush felt that 'Nicko always looked like an unmade bed'.[c] His carefully cultivated eccentricity endeared him to Washington, as did lavish entertainment at the Residence overseen by his wife Mary. 'The Embassy always buzzed', said Anson. 'They gave fantastic parties mixing the political elite, celebrities and business leaders.'[d] Bridging the Carter and Reagan administrations, Henderson built exceptionally strong links to both.

Henderson also proved adept at public relations. First, he befriended opinion formers in Washington: Katharine Graham, owner and publisher of the *The Washington Post*, became a regular partner on the Residence's tennis court. More importantly, Henderson was a gifted performer on television: 'I may one day come unstuck', he wrote in his diary, 'but at the moment the telly seems one of the easiest PR activities one can take part in.'[e] In fact, Henderson never did come 'unstuck'. Harnessing the building and his own diplomatic skill, Henderson was able to make a real impact in Washington and, particularly during the difficult days of the Falklands War, help keep London and Washington on the same page.

RIGHT President Reagan talks with 'Nicko' Henderson in the Drawing Room prior to dinner at the Residence on 27 February 1981. Engaged in a heartfelt discussion of Californian wine, Reagan opined that such wine would benefit from extended cellaring. Whether the President enjoyed the 1974 Robert Mondavi Cabernet Sauvignon served with dinner is not recorded.

Margaret and Ron: A Political Love Affair

Ronald Reagan and Margaret Thatcher were ideological soulmates: both wanted radical economic reform at home and, fearing the West was losing the Cold War, a more aggressive posture abroad. 'We'll lend strength to each other', Reagan pledged when Thatcher called him the day after his inauguration. 'We will', she replied.[8] A little over a month later, Thatcher became the first European head of government to visit Reagan in Washington.

Thatcher's visit, in February 1981, was not popular with everyone in the Reagan administration. With the British economy still in dire straits, officials feared Reagan, who shared Thatcher's economic approach, would be tainted by association. The president, however, rejected such timidity and instructed aides to make the visit special. The occasion, wrote the national security advisor, Richard Allen, would 'dramatize ... a meeting of minds which encompasses not only philosophical affinities ... but also a tough, pragmatic determination to do something about them'.[9]

With his own vision to 'dramatize the meeting of minds', Henderson played fast and loose. A grand dinner at the White House was to be followed by a return engagement at the Residence, with the vice president the guest of honour. Slyly, Henderson suggested to Allen early on that the president might also attend. Allen agreed and Henderson swiftly sent out invitations. Only later did

the Americans realise that this was a gross breach of protocol: the president never attended return dinners at embassies unless the visitor was a head of state. Thatcher was merely a head of government. 'Allen telephoned me to try to get me to say that I had pulled a fast one', Henderson recorded.[10] But the dinner was now a fait accompli and the administration embraced it.

On 27 February, the Reagans duly dined at the Residence. The wine was Californian, the atmosphere electric and the bonhomie unmistakable: 'truly a warm & beautiful occasion', Reagan wrote in his diary. 'I believe a real friendship exists between the P.M. her family & us.'[11] Thatcher felt the same. At the bottom of her thank you letter to Reagan she scribbled: 'We shall never have a happier visit.'[12]

In February 1985 (this time during the tenure of Henderson's successor, Sir Oliver Wright), Reagan was again invited to the Residence. In light of the president's relationship with Thatcher, the National Security Council (NSC) counselled acceptance and Reagan happily threw protocol to the wind once more. While most embassies yearned for even a brief presidential appearance, the Reagans' willingness to visit 3100 Massachusetts Avenue was a mark of just how close Anglo-American relations had become.

The success of Reagan's visits helped reinforce Thatcher's instinctive liking for Lutyens' building. During her early visits,

FACING PAGE The setting for President Reagan's first dinner at the Residence, on 27 February 1981. Luring the president to the Embassy was a mark of his respect for Thatcher and a real triumph for the political nous of 'Nicko' Henderson.
RIGHT President Reagan takes evident delight in Thatcher's dinner toast at the Residence on 20 February 1985: 'We in Britain think you are a wonderful President', she told Reagan, who had recently won re-election, 'and from one old hand to another, welcome to a second term!'

as leader of the opposition, her style had proved a shock to the Residence. She liked 'to be active from a very early hour', said Peter Jay, who recalled noises emerging from her private quarters, 'often to do with the performance or non-performance of her hairdresser'.[13] In later years, Thatcher grew fond of the Residence, often relaxing in the Library over a glass of whisky. 'I think she regarded it as a bit of a home away from home', recalled Lord Powell, her private secretary for foreign affairs. 'Because of her predisposition towards America, she felt more comfortable there than anywhere else in the world.'[14] Whenever the Treasury sought to cut back on Britain's grand buildings overseas, the ambassador could always rely on the support of the prime minister. Her argument was simple: 'you cannot put a price on prestige'.[15]

In the early 1980s, Britain and America once again had leaders with close personal ties and shared national interests. Reagan and Thatcher employed tough rhetoric towards the Soviet Union and worked to enhance NATO's nuclear deterrent by deploying new US missiles to Europe. They also collaborated at international summits, often defending their shared economic radicalism: 'Margaret Thatcher not only helped Reagan learn the ropes, but was the right flank', said close Reagan aide, Michael Deaver.[16] But the real test came in April 1982, when Argentina invaded the Falkland Islands, a British colony in the South Atlantic.

With the unprovoked Argentine occupation of British soil on 2 April 1982, Thatcher was disappointed not to receive Reagan's immediate and wholehearted support. Instead, valuing its relations with Latin America, the administration chose to mediate: the United States had to 'get these two brawlers out of the bar room', Reagan told his officials. But he added a crucial bottom line: 'our first order of business, if worst comes to worst, is to side

with the Brits'.[17] Sure enough, when Argentine intransigence led negotiations to break down, America swung behind Britain. Although some officials continued to push Britain towards compromise, the Pentagon now stepped up the provision of vital military materiel.

For the Embassy, building American public support was crucial and Henderson took to the airwaves with aplomb. Embassy officials lobbied their administration contacts as the ambassador worked on the top players, including Caspar Weinberger, Reagan's anglophile secretary of defence. So successful were these efforts that, during a walk with Henderson in the Residence garden, Weinberger offered to lease Britain a US aircraft carrier for the duration of the conflict.[18] That the offer proved impractical did not detract from its generosity.

After bitter fighting, Argentine forces surrendered to British troops on 14 June. A big party followed at the Residence, with US officials who had been unhelpful carefully eliminated from the guest list. Reagan and Thatcher had not always been on precisely the same page, but the Americans had provided support when it really mattered, making a major contribution to Britain's victory. This was something Thatcher would never forget.

At the end of July 1982, Henderson retired for a second (and final) time. His replacement was Sir Oliver Wright. A professional diplomat, like Henderson plucked out of retirement, Wright was a jovial character with a quarterdeck manner. While not a master of detail, his easy-going manner won him admirers when he arrived in Washington that summer. 'The overwhelming impression is one of great friendliness', Wright reported. 'Britain's reputation here, due certainly to our Falklands performance, but by no means only to it, is high.'[19]

Unfortunately Wright's own reputation suffered following an early faux pas with George Shultz, the secretary of state. Protesting a US tilt to the Argentinean position on the Falklands, albeit months after the conflict ended, Wright demanded to see Shultz and 'read me off like a sergeant would a recruit in a Marine Corps boot camp'.[20] Livid, Shultz refused to see Wright again for some time, a fact Embassy officials endeavoured to hide from London.

Wright was not alone in experiencing difficulties with the Americans. In October 1983, for example, the United States invaded Grenada, a member of the British Commonwealth, without consulting Britain. Thatcher, stung by accusations that she lacked influence in Washington, condemned the action publicly. Reagan now trod carefully. 'If I were there Margaret, I'd throw my hat in the door before I came in', he said, evoking the imagery of a saloon in the Wild West when he called to apologise.[21] The crisis soon passed. Reagan and Thatcher had their eyes on a greater prize: victory in the Cold War.

In the early 1980s, Thatcher and Reagan had built up Western military strength. Thatcher now sought to persuade Reagan to engage with Mikhail Gorbachev, Soviet leader from 1985. Meeting him in 1984, she had famously declared: 'I like Mr Gorbachev. We can do business together.'[22] With her reputation as a cold warrior on the line, Reagan eventually followed her lead. A rash of international summitry ensued, helping to defuse tension. Thatcher also helped persuade Reagan to back Gorbachev's domestic reforms, which eventually, albeit unintentionally, helped bring about the end of the Soviet Union.

Throughout this period, Thatcher kept a wary eye on Reagan. Meeting Gorbachev at Reykjavik, in October 1986, the president came close to agreeing to eliminate all nuclear weapons. Thatcher was appalled. Europe still relied on these weapons as the ultimate defence against Moscow's overwhelming conventional forces. And now Reagan was willing to give them away? It was, she said later, 'the only time when I really have felt the ground shake under my feet'.[23] But her relationship with Reagan was such that she visited him a few weeks later and persuaded him to put the idea on the back burner.

Britain was now punching above its weight in world affairs in a way not seen for years. Thatcher, in one sense, had assumed the role of intermediary so coveted by Macmillan. But her concept of intermediary was neither patronising nor impartial. Much as she liked Gorbachev, her allegiance lay with Reagan and an unshakeable Anglo-American partnership.

The Bush Era: A Course Adjustment

In January 1989, George H. W. Bush succeeded Reagan as president. The ambassador, by this time, was Sir Antony Acland, who had succeeded Wright in August 1986. Unusually, Acland had arrived in Washington a widower, having lost his wife two years previously. This caught the attention of George Bush, then vice president, whose residence was adjacent to the Embassy. Bush telephoned Acland, soon after his arrival in Washington, and invited him to 'hop over the garden fence to come and have a drink'.[24] Acland responded that, if he did so, he would probably be shot by the Secret Service, so he would prefer to use the main entrance. Many such visits followed and Acland quickly established a very friendly relationship with Bush and his wife Barbara. As a widower, Acland also attracted interest amongst Washington society. According to Barbara Bush, 'everyone was trying to find a bride for him. Smart man as he was, he went home and found wonderful Jenny', instead.[25] They were married in 1987.

As couples the Aclands and Bushes became very close, even as the latter entered the White House. The president had acquired a taste for Chinese food during his time as ambassador in Beijing and would on occasion invite the Aclands for dinner at a Chinese restaurant or to see a movie at the White House. This relationship, however, was a personal one, which usually steered clear of politics. When the press, or even Embassy officials, asked Acland what had been discussed he replied simply that these were private occasions between friends and he had nothing to say about them at all.[26]

By early 1989, the mood music between London and Washington was positive. The Acland-Bush relationship reinforced this, as did Thatcher's personal ties to Bush, whom she had cultivated as vice president. London confidently expected continuity.

Bush also believed in strong Anglo-American ties and he liked Thatcher personally: 'we felt very close to Margaret and I was especially close to Denis', his wife recalled.[27] Critically, however, the new president felt that Reagan had allowed Thatcher too much influence. He felt the relationship needed a course correction: 'I had to speak for myself.'[28]

While Thatcher struggled to adapt to this new style, more substantive problems emerged. For one, the Bush administration now sought a closer partnership with Germany, which left relations with Britain diminished. After the fall of the Berlin Wall, in October 1989, this led to considerable tension. While Bush supported Germany's growing desire to unify, Thatcher disagreed. She felt that losing East Germany could be a mortal blow to Gorbachev, threatening the peaceful transition to democracy in Eastern Europe. She also feared a more powerful Germany. 'Whenever she would talk about German unification', recalled Condoleezza Rice, then an NSC staffer, 'Thatcher would bristle, recalling how the Germans had sent her family scurrying into bomb shelters when she was child.'[29] This was not a ripe period for Anglo-American collaboration.

Everything changed after Saddam Hussein invaded Kuwait in August 1990. A shared determination to stand up to the Iraqi dictator, while mitigating the threat to Middle Eastern oil, brought Britain and America back together. Although Thatcher had less patience for working through the United Nations than the Americans, she supported their efforts publicly and committed thousands of British troops. In November 1990, she lost office, but her successor John Major forged his own relationship with Bush, which soon became a firm friendship. Together they saw the Gulf crisis through, forcing Saddam's forces out of Kuwait by the end of February 1991.

Coda: More Recent Times

WITH THE COLD WAR AT AN END, A QUESTION MARK HUNG over Anglo-American relations. Collaboration over nuclear weapons and shared intelligence continued but the question increasingly came to be asked to what end? How would the 'special relationship' adapt to the new era, when it was no longer sustained by the struggle against communism?

The answer, during the 1990s, was unclear. When the breakup of Yugoslavia led to armed conflict in 1992, the response in London and Washington was divided. Britain was not enthusiastic about a military entanglement, insisting that the Serb campaign of 'ethnic cleansing' against Bosnia's Muslims was part of an intractable civil war. Bush agreed. After Bill Clinton became president in 1993, however, American pressure to act on behalf of the Bosnians grew. Difficult and protracted negotiations followed, reaching agreement on joint US-UK participation in NATO airstrikes against the Bosnian Serbs only in 1995, before the US-led Dayton talks brought the conflict to a close at the end of the year.

Politically, Major and Clinton were never going to be soulmates. Northern Ireland offered another persistent irritant in their relationship. Previous administrations had kept out of the issue, but Clinton chose to put his finger on the Irish Republican side of the scale. His decision, in 1994, to grant Sinn Fein's Gerry Adams a US visa, against London's vehement opposition and before an IRA ceasefire was in place, infuriated Major, as did the decision the following year to allow Adams to raise funds for Sinn Fein in America. Towards the end of Major's time in office, he and Clinton drew closer together in the pursuit of peace but it took a change of prime minister to bring this issue to fruition.

With the election of Tony Blair, in May 1997, a personal friendship returned to US-UK ties. Blair and Clinton shared a desire to reinvigorate the centre-left. In office they worked closely on most issues – both deserve credit for bringing about the 1998 Good Friday Agreement in Northern Ireland – but they did not always see eye-to-eye.

Blair now became wedded to military intervention in the Balkans on humanitarian grounds. In 1999, RAF Tornadoes joined US aircraft in launching airstrikes aimed at stopping Slobodan Milosevic's ethnic cleansing in Kosovo. When this appeared ineffective, Blair urged Clinton to commit ground troops. Clinton resisted, arguing that neither European governments nor American public opinion would support this major escalation. For all Blair's passion, much of any troop commitment would have to be American. Britain was already punching above its weight: this was a step too far. Fortunately, the threat of boots on the ground proved sufficient for Milosevic to fold.

The attacks of 11 September 2001 (9/11) provided Britain and America with a powerful new shared interest: the struggle against Islamic terrorism. While America had been attacked, Britain too had suffered: sixty-seven of those killed that day were British. Blair crossed the Atlantic nine days later and was present as guest of honour of the new president, George W. Bush, when he addressed a special joint session of Congress: 'America has no truer friend than Great Britain', Bush proclaimed as he declared war on Al Qaeda and global terrorism. 'Once again, we are joined together in a great cause.'[1] Blair's presence there, and at Ground Zero the next day, was a powerful gesture that lingered in the American mind in the months and years that followed.

Even before 9/11, Blair had established a good relationship with Bush. This now grew much tighter. Both Bush and Blair were determined to pursue Al Qaeda, which would require military

LEFT President Bush and Prime Minister Blair in Crawford, Texas, in April 2002, following a meeting at the president's ranch. Blair insisted that Britain would support an invasion of Iraq subject to certain conditions, but over the months that followed those 'conditions' lost much of their force. **FACING PAGE, TOP, LEFT** Prime Minister Brown and Senator Barack Obama on 17 April 2008. **FACING PAGE, TOP, RIGHT** Prime Minister Cameron and President Hollande getting acquainted on 18 May 2012. **FACING PAGE, BOTTOM** Former President Clinton and former Secretary of State Hillary Clinton in the Ambassador's Study with Sir Peter Westmacott and Lady Westmacott in November 2013. President Clinton declared, 'If I had the good fortune to live in this house, I'd never leave this room.'

action against the Taliban in Afghanistan, a terrorist safe haven. Blair helped persuade Bush to seek broad international support for military action. Anglo-American relations were at the forefront of world affairs once again. The military action against Afghanistan proved an initial success, although the longer term stability of the country proved a more difficult proposition.

In 2003, Britain and America again fought side by side during the controversial invasion of Iraq. Presented to the public as a war to remove the threat from Saddam Hussein's weapons of mass destruction (WMD), the discovery that no such WMD existed undermined the war's rationale. For Blair and Bush, the morality of removing a brutal dictator from power was reason enough, but the chaos that ensued in post-war Iraq, and huge loss of life, left many unconvinced. Others questioned why Blair was unable to persuade the United States to make more progress in the Middle East peace process, an oft-stated goal in London. While in many ways a highpoint for cooperation, Iraq also showed the limits to British influence.

Alongside visible action, Britain and America worked closely to combat terrorism behind the scenes. When, in 2005, London's 7/7 (7 July) bombings left fifty-two people dead, President Bush was at a G8 meeting in Scotland. Blair left early to return to London. On Bush's return to the US, he drove straight to the British Embassy to sign the book of condolence. It was a significant gesture of solidarity in a struggle that is likely to remain at the forefront of Anglo-American relations for years to come.

Today the Residence continues to attract individuals of the highest calibre. In April 2008, Prime Minister Gordon Brown met then-candidate Barack Obama at the house. In May 2012, the new French president, François Hollande, who knew the am-

bassador, Sir Peter Westmacott, from his time in Paris, made the unusual gesture of calling on Prime Minister David Cameron at the Residence for their first-ever meeting. In early 2013, former President Bill Clinton, Hillary Clinton and Chelsea Clinton were there for the last dinner Hillary Clinton attended as secretary of state. So the Residence continues to serve the cause of Anglo-American friendship today just as strongly as it did when Edwin Lutyens fashioned it for a very different era.

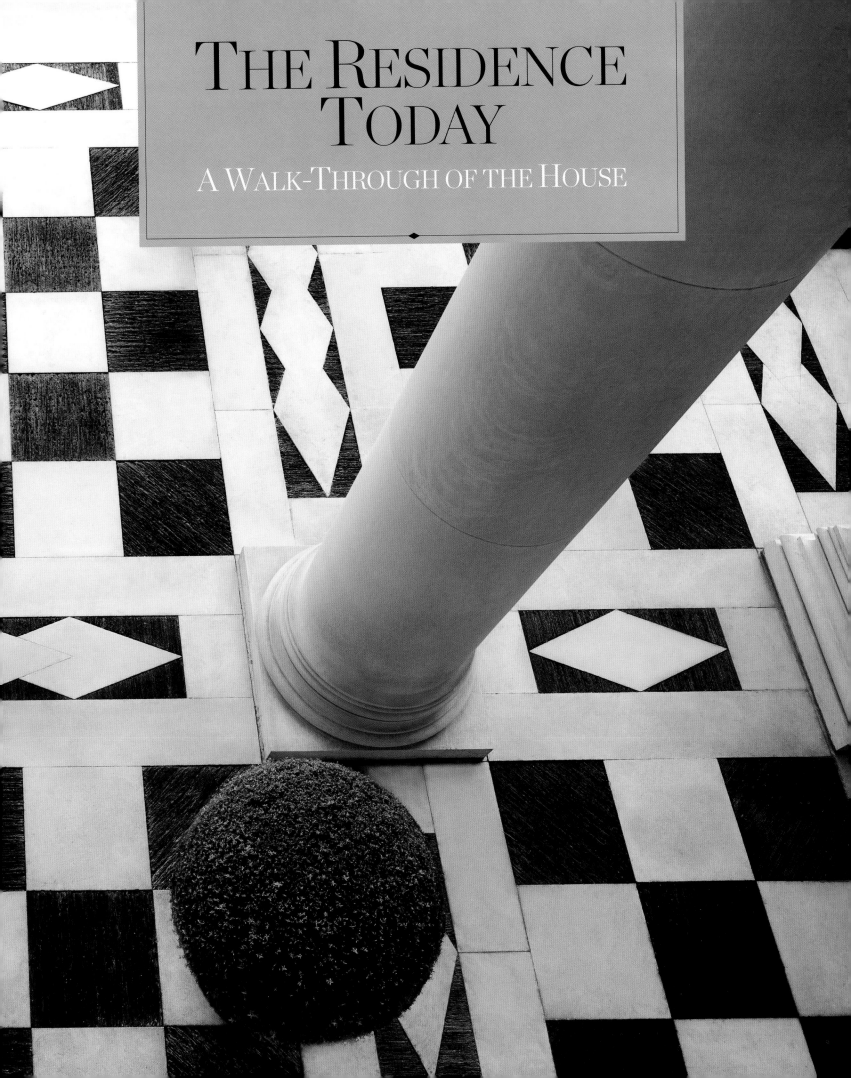

THE RESIDENCE TODAY

A WALK-THROUGH OF THE HOUSE

A Marriage of British
and American Architecture

The Residence is a beautiful place and it came from the Imperial Era. There is a gravitas about the Embassy and your ambassadors use it well. It makes a big difference if you have an Embassy that is some kind of artistic expression, which therefore recalls the country's eminence. The British Embassy is beautifully organised inside, to entertain, for discussions, or for a presentation. I think its design has a great impact ... certainly, nobody could consider it a hardship to go to the British Embassy.

Dr Henry Kissinger, US Secretary of State, 1973–7

Lutyens' British Embassy, comprising the Residence and Chancery, is one of his finest buildings and one of the most strikingly beautiful purpose-built diplomatic buildings in the world. It is the equal, aesthetically and functionally, of the Viceroy's House in New Delhi that was completed at the same time as the Embassy was first inhabited in 1930.

The Embassy's style is closely related to the most obviously Classical of Lutyens' late pre-war country houses such as Great Maytham (1909) and The Salutations (1911), both in Kent. Sir Christopher Wren (1632–1723) was a strong influence, and the Embassy is reminiscent of his Royal Chelsea Hospital in London, which Lutyens described as: 'one of Wren's best and most dignified buildings'.[1] Lutyens successfully blended this very English style with the eighteenth-century domestic architecture found in Colonial America, where one sees the influence of the remarkable sixteenth-century Italian architect, Andrea Palladio. Flourishes from Palladio's work appear in several eighteenth-century American buildings, including at Williamsburg, Monticello, Mount Vernon and in Virginian plantation houses.

In the early days, the Washington Embassy met with an enthusiastic contemporary reception from the Commission for Fine Arts in Washington and from the press. Before it was even completed, *The Washington Post* described it in December 1929 as: 'the finest Embassy in the world. A home fit for a king, or for the President of the United States ... An ornament to Washington, the Capital of the greatest nation on earth. What a contribution to making Washington the finest capital in the world!'[2]

The External Elevations and the Main Gates

The first visitors see of the Embassy is the Old Chancery facing Massachusetts Avenue. Putting an extra floor on top of each wing, a late addition at Howard's urging to provide extra office space, creates the impression of a tall narrowness. Considered 'un-American' by some contemporary critics, many others admired the more imposing presence it gave the building from the road.

The Chancery's narrow verticality is further accentuated by the steeply-pitched roofs, with tall chimneys, a conscious imitation of Wren's distinctive chimneys at the Chelsea Hospital, London. The height further served a particular architectural purpose in Washington. As Christopher Hussey, the architectural editor at *Country Life*, a magazine that so supported Lutyens, put it: the height of the Chancery wings 'illustrate Lutyens' axiom that, that in a design on a sloping site, dominating mass is required for the lower level'.[3]

Lutyens loved to build in bricks – narrow two-inch was his preferred height. Procurement of these bricks from Virginia, and limestone from Vermont, led to several delays during construction but was crucial to the effect Lutyens was seeking to achieve. Their small size helps to accentuate the scale of the building, one of many visual tricks he commonly deployed. Lutyens was a master of geometry and perspective.

ABOVE This drawing by Cyril Farey clearly shows the land rising upwards from the road, with the Residence behind on higher ground. The last minute addition of the extra floor to the Chancery in the foreground allowed Lutyens to give the Embassy a much more prominent presence from the street.

The roofs are supported by a very deep and strongly moulded cornice, better described as a frieze, which does not project outwards. To keep the junction of roof and frieze free of guttering, Lutyens came up with a device he had used before: a concealed gutter above the eves. While most of the Chancery has a flat roof, Lutyens maintains the steeply pitched roof on the Residence behind it, again to help emphasise its physical scale and presence.

Passers-by might assume that this view of the Chancery from the road was intended to be the grandest. But Lutyens is full of surprises. He liked his principal rooms wherever possible to face south, towards the gardens, and that is exactly where he places his most impressive façade: facing south over the garden, rather than eastwards towards the road. For visitors, this device provides a startling revelation. As *The New York Times* put it in October 1930: 'critics laughingly observed Lutyens has put his front door at the back and his back door at the front', but added, 'they are right. It is the instinct of the British to conceal their façade and no one looking at the Embassy from the street could have any idea of the more majestic portions of an exterior which is viewed from the garden.'[4]

The façade and Main Gates from the road in fact display the genius of Lutyens as an architect. The original plot of land narrowed to only an opening of less than 200 feet onto Massachusetts Avenue before broadening out. The slope of the land directly away from the road to the west meant the far side of the plot was a full twenty-three feet higher. Lutyens thus decided to place the bulk of his structure north of the main east-west axis to obtain the maximum garden area in the south. This ensured that the new Embassy would enjoy a sweeping view towards downtown Washington, taking in both the Potomac River Valley and the Capitol (now obscured by trees).

The daily volume of visitors and staff passing in and out of the Chancery further dictated Lutyens' decision to place the Chancery nearest to the road, and to put the more elegant, spacious Residence behind it. Had the land immediately to the south, purchased in 1931, been available when Lutyens was planning the building, he might well have planned it in an entirely different way. But who is to say it would have been a better building?

BELOW This sectional drawing, looking westwards, shows a view of the *Porte-Cochère* with the Residence behind but without the Chancery that stands in front.

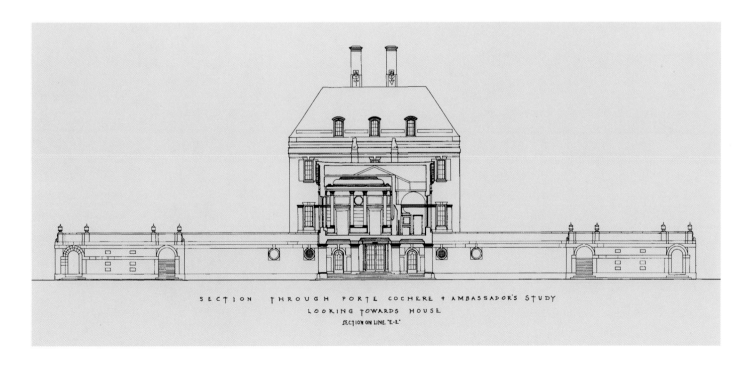

SECTION THROUGH PORTE COCHERE + AMBASSADOR'S STUDY
LOOKING TOWARDS HOUSE
SECTION ON LINE "E-E."

ABOVE Lutyens celebrated intricate and powerfully symbolic statues, as an integral part of his whole design. He placed the unicorn and crowned lion statues seen here above the Main Gates on Massachusetts Avenue leading to the Residence. **FACING PAGE** The Main Floor plan shows the three-sided Chancery building at the bottom and the Residence behind.

Cars were still relatively in their infancy in the 1920s, but Lutyens knew that both Chancery and Residence would require fast-flowing entrances and exits on to Massachusetts Avenue. How could he manage this without it looking cluttered? His design at the Viceroy's House provided the solution. In New Delhi, he had built a carriage-way *under* the structure of the house for the rapid depositing and collecting of large numbers of guests on ceremonial occasions. In Washington, he built four gates on the road, the outer pair serving the Residence, and the inner pair the Chancery only. The Residence gates are each adorned by a lion and a unicorn, while urns are set atop the Chancery gateposts.

The Chancery itself forms three sides of a quadrangle with the fourth side open to Massachusetts Avenue. Lutyens used almost the entire width available to him for the building, bar the space for the driveways to and from the Residence. The Chancery drive originally formed a sweeping U-shape, planted in between with grass, but with the demands of modern life, it has become a car park.

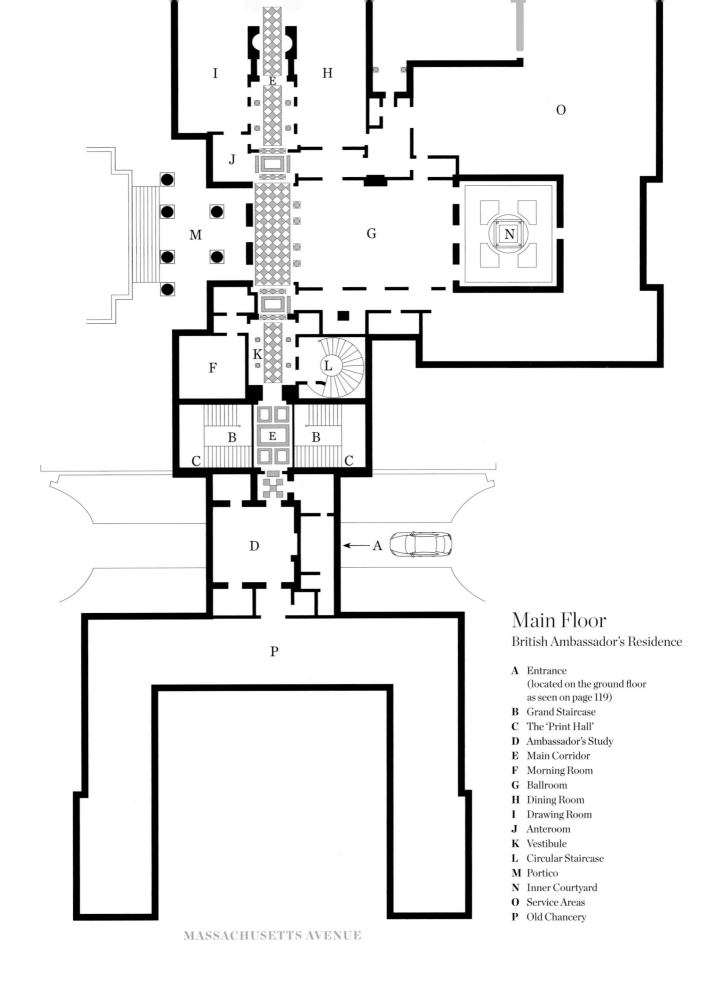

Main Floor
Brit** Ambassador's Residence

A Entrance
(located on the ground floor
as seen on page 119)

B Grand Staircase

C The 'Print Hall'

D Ambassador's Study

E Main Corridor

F Morning Room

G Ballroom

H Dining Room

I Drawing Room

J Anteroom

K Vestibule

L Circular Staircase

M Portico

N Inner Courtyard

O Service Areas

P Old Chancery

MASSACHUSETTS AVENUE

Lutyens' Architectural Vocabulary

Lutyens had an irrepressible sense of humour which flowed through his speech and letters into his buildings. The Embassy reflects the quirky nature of his humour, where he parodies architectural styles and even himself. Examples include the children's 'spy' window in the Morning Room, his capitals without columns, and impressively grand doors that open only to very shallow cupboards. The Embassy's architectural wit has been commented upon widely throughout the years, and it has done much to endear the building to its visitors. *The New York Times* went so far as to say the Embassy displayed 'England's fondness for freaks'.[5] These two pages also display Lutyens' extraordinary ambition as an architect, designing fine details of carving but also fixtures and fittings in and outside the building, such as the elegant geometric lights opposite.

One of the delights of Lutyens as an architect is the minute attention that he gives to decorative work.

FACING PAGE (FROM LEFT TO RIGHT) A detail from the west façade; One of a pair of lions carved in an Art Deco style that sit atop the Ambassador's Study.

BELOW A detail from the column to the left of the west door of the Residence.

RIGHT A remarkable carving from the front of the *Porte-Cochère* that displays Lutyens' penchant for using traditional elements in a modernist manner, here blending naturalistic flowers with a stylised head.

BOTTOM Two examples of regal light fixtures designed by Lutyens that adorn the exterior walls of the Residence and the Old Chancery.

The Porte-Cochère

Disregarding the slope, Lutyens decided to keep the driveway to the Residence flat. The ground floor entrance to the Residence is on the same level as the Chancery's first floor. Above the entrance, the Chancery is connected to the Residence by a bridge, or *Porte-Cochère*, on which, as a masterstroke, Lutyens placed the Ambassador's Study. On the parapet for this linking bridge, Lutyens placed stone lions, arranging for the model of the lion on the First World War monument at Nieuport in Belgium to be sent to Washington.[6]

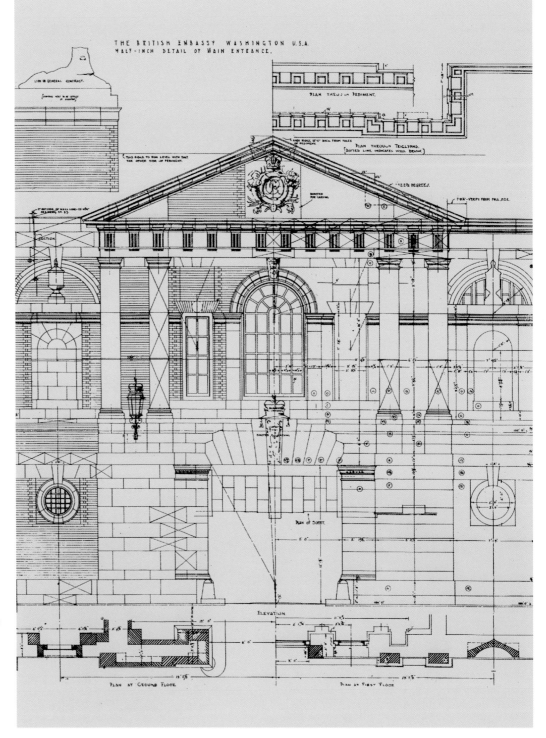

PAGES 116–17 Lutyens placed this pediment, with its royal crest and British flag, over the Ambassador's Study, which serves as a bridge connecting the Chancery and Residence. Placing the Study here provides a link between the more formal representative functions of the Residence and the office work carried out in the Chancery.

RIGHT This drawing offers a keen sense of the meticulous detail with which Lutyens designed all of his buildings.

FACING PAGE The *Porte-Cochère* as it is today, revealing the narrow aperture through which cars and carriages might travel to drop off or collect visitors.

Entry Hall and Grand Staircase

The main entrance to the Residence under the *Porte-Cochère* evokes stern officialdom, without any suggestion of what lies upstairs. Passing through the main doors into the Entry Hall, visitors encounter a dramatic plain stone arch above and geometrically arranged floor tiles below, drawing them to the foot of the Grand Staircase illuminated, on either side, by light from the open space above.

This double staircase, sweeping out expansively to the south and north, is as theatrical as it is imposing. Lutyens wanted visitors to sense that something grand and special awaited them above. The balustrade is particularly striking: a series of stepped lines run along its top, which catch the eye and incline the visitors upwards. Using a favoured Lutyens device, the ironwork of the staircase mimics the movement of the stairs, which are constructed of limestone from Indiana. This ironwork contains strong echoes of the Lutyens staircase at the now destroyed Cheyne Walk house he designed in London.

At the top of the stairs lies the main east-west axis of the building. Lutyens wanted visitors to be awed by the long vista that now greeted them, and achieved this, in part, by employing imposing entablature to the left and right of the doorframes without the pilasters (slightly projected columns) that many would expect.

FACING PAGE Under the *Porte-Cochère*, visitors mount seven wide steps to the entrance doors, above which Lutyens has placed a carved cherub, similar to those in Sir Christopher Wren's St Paul's Cathedral, London. **BELOW** The view from the Entry Hall looking out towards the *Porte-Cochère*. Lutyens deliberately employs a very restricted palette of colours, of greys and whites, in his superbly proportioned hallway, whose flooring is full of geometric patterning.

The 'Print Hall'

Devised and hung by the UK Government Art Collection in April 2012, the 'Print Hall' is a contemporary interpretation of the print rooms that were fashionable in British country houses in the late eighteenth and early nineteenth centuries, made by pasting prints of various subjects on to walls in symmetrical patterns. These were sometimes 'framed' by engraved mouldings, the choice of prints and patterns becoming a unique monument to the maker's interests and tastes. Very few such print rooms now survive.

Rather than being pasted on to the walls of three sides of the Grand Staircase, the one hundred and eighteen prints in the display have been framed and glazed, their black, gold and black-gold frames complementing the colour scheme of the Staircase balustrade. Featuring portraits, country houses, botanical specimens, animals, views of London, cathedrals, churches, castles and 'fancy pictures', the prints reflect several themes connected with the Residence, its architecture and the United States.

One print depicts Sir Christopher Wren's Chelsea Hospital in London, an inspiration for much Colonial American architecture and also at least in part for Lutyens' design for the Residence. Within the display is a portrait of the architect, and several allusions to the building's carefully-designed symmetry. At the top of the spaces between the two central windows are two early 1780s oval engravings of Windsor Castle from the north west and south east, the same axis upon which the Residence was built. There are also references to Pierre L'Enfant's designs for the city of Washington that were inspired by formal baroque landscape and city design as seen in the gardens of the Palace of Versailles in France. Some of the gardens depicted feature tree-lined avenues radiating from central points interspersed with half circles, circles and pools, as for example in the two prints of Hampton Court Palace and of Leyton Grange, which are themselves hung diagonally opposite each other in the display. Such formality had long dominated European garden design, and is seen in several 'birds-eye views' of English gardens which in turn pay homage to the modern horticultural achievements of the Residence gardens.

PAGES 122-3 Lutyens always conceived of his buildings in three dimensions, in contrast to the modernist placing of function ahead of form. Nowhere in the Residence is his mastery of dimension and his generous use of space seen to better effect than in the dazzling Grand Staircase. Lutyens employed a similar double staircase design at the Viceroy's House in New Delhi, with a large space above open to the sky.

ABOVE Lutyens' design for the wrought iron balustrade for the Grand Staircase, 1925.

FACING PAGE Dating from 1898 and with over 13,500 works of art spanning five centuries, the UK Government Art Collection is the most dispersed collection of British art in the world. Placed in offices and official residences, the Collection helps promote British art and history while contributing to cultural diplomacy.

The popularity of print rooms coincided with the reigns of King George III and his son King George IV, whose portraits – as well as those of other members of the Hanoverian family – are featured, along with those of people of fashion after paintings by leading artists in the late eighteenth and nineteenth centuries, including the American-born second President of the Royal Academy, Benjamin West. A number of engraved portrait heads are seen in three prints positioned in a triangle on the main display to the left of the gallery which commemorate three British naval victories during the Napoleonic wars. The appearance of these heads is echoed in the work of contemporary British artist Julian Opie in a pair of portraits at the centre of the two main hangs, *Luc and Ludivine get Married* from 2007. Comprising laser-cut paper in oval frames designed by the artist, the works are inspired by the eighteenth and nineteenth century fashions for silhouettes and cameos, the portraits conceived in the artist's signature style of reducing facial features down to a bare minimum.

At the base of each symmetrical display are four black-and-white prints, including a portrait of Arthur Wellesley, 1st Duke of Wellington. This is a reminder of how the Duke, a great enthusiast for print rooms, placed portraits of himself in prominent positions in the examples he designed for his country house, Stratfield Saye, in Hampshire, even as the fashion for this type of interior decoration was waning.

JULIA TOFFOLO, *UK Government Art Collection*

FACING PAGE Buildings of Classical inspiration, flora and fauna and bird's-eye views of long-lost formal gardens are amongst the 118 prints in the 'Print Hall' display. Amongst them is a portrait of Lutyens himself.
RIGHT The 'Print Hall' is a dramatic introduction to the Residence for visitors, who are inevitably attracted by the symmetrical patterns of the display and the variety of subjects.
PAGES 128-9 The view of the Main Corridor at the top of the staircase, which provides an imposing entrance to the Ambassador's Study ahead. Lutyens has, in fact, created two bridges in his building: the bridge containing the Ambassador's Study over the entrance to the Residence, and the bridge from which this photograph is taken.

Ambassador's Study

The Ambassador's Study, also called the Library, placed over the bridge, enjoys views through the Palladian windows to the south. If any Lutyens room can be said to approach perfection, surely this is it. Almost a cube, the room has a deeply coved ceiling emphasising its height. The perfect symmetry suggests a room of power and substance. Lutyens specially selected liquidambar, a form of gum tree that thrives in California, for the light brown wooden panelling, which looks particularly striking as the morning light streams in through the windows.

Great attention is given to the detailed carving of the wood, executed with superb craftsmanship. The carved pilasters on all four walls have Corinthian capitals. Between them is a periodic richly carved frieze, which recalls the Mannerist inventions of Michelangelo and other sixteenth-century architects. This foreshadows the friezes in the 'Print Hall' and in the Ballroom. Lutyens places periodic wreaths with keystones at the base, a reference to the more traditional wreaths in limestone that ornament the outer walls of the building. The room boasts a most impressive fireplace, with a white marble mantel that recalls the Viceroy's House. In New Delhi, he placed a stylised circular wooden panel above the mantel; here he left a space to hang a portrait.

Lutyens was unable to use the large mahogany doors from the former British Embassy in Connecticut Avenue, despite pleas from Howard. But he gives the Study six doors, all made from liquidambar. Some lead to cupboards or a washroom, while the two most important connect the Study with the Chancery to the east, and to the Main Corridor through the Residence to the west.

FACING PAGE Lutyens was rarely generous in the space that he provided for the hanging of paintings, but one such space exists over the fireplace in the Ambassador's Study. Here hangs the oil portrait, *Sir Winston Leonard Spencer Churchill*, painted by Julian Lamar (1893–1967) after the famous photograph by Yousuf Karsh of 1941.
RIGHT The sitting area in the middle of the Ambassador's Study. On the right lies the ambassador's desk and through the windows in the early days could be seen views of the Capitol and the city of Washington.
PAGES 132–3 Lutyens designed every facet of these intricately carved walls. The height of the room can be comprehended by noting the scale of the doors. The portrait of Field Marshal Montgomery, painted in 1952 by Eisenhower, his colleague (and rival) during the Second World War, is hung in front of the book case. The painting was presented to the Embassy in 1970 by Walter Annenberg, a distinguished American ambassador to Britain.

Lutyens loved to make a feature of long corridors in his domestic houses, even to the detriment of space for habitable areas at the Residence. Any loss of space is more than compensated by the elegance of the Main Corridor and its visual delights. Castle Drogo (Devon, 1930) and Gledstone Hall (North Yorkshire, 1927) feature similar corridors. The latter's black-and-white floor pattern is strikingly similar to that of the Main Corridor at the Residence – unsurprisingly as it was nearing completion as Lutyens was designing the Embassy.

The Main Corridor is a shade under 165 feet from end to end. It is one of Lutyens' most successful Residence features and it adorns the cover of this book. Its very length would have daunted lesser architects, but becomes a tour de force here as Lutyens cleverly varies the width and the play of light. From the Ambassador's Study, the corridor opens out on both sides as it crosses over the Grand Staircase, then narrows between the anterooms and the private staircase to the bedroom floor, widens out again as it passes the Ballroom and doors to the Portico, before narrowing finally by the Drawing Room and the Dining Room at the far end.

Lutyens was remarkably sensitive to light, and how it played at different times of day and in different seasons. The bright natural light from the large glass doors onto the Portico and garden thus deliberately contrasts with the darker parts of the corridor, which he lights with chandeliers. True to the Arts and Crafts Movement's preference for natural materials, he eschewed carpets and put great effort into building bare floors with often geometric designs in contrasting colours. The Main Corridor's diagonal squares are made of Vermont marble and Pennsylvania slate. The size of the squares is slightly larger at the far end, another of several devices to enhance the sense of perspective.

RIGHT Lutyens loved designing long dramatic corridors, using a series of entrances and intervening spaces to provide variety and differing experiences of light. On this page the Main Corridor from the bridge in front of the Ambassador's Study towards the west doorway. The square floor tiles at the far or west end are larger, one of his many tricks of perspective.

FACING PAGE View of the Main Corridor from the west door back towards and through the Ambassador's Study to the window at the far end at the east façade of the Old Chancery. On either side of the Corridor are bronze busts of Lionel Percy Smythe by Sir Alfred Gilbert (left) and Sir Alfred J. Munnings by Edwin Whitney-Smith (right), on loan from the Royal Academy of Arts, London.

Morning Room

The Morning Room is the first main door on the left along the Main Corridor. On Lutyens' original plan, it is described as the 'Library', but ambassadors have used it as a family sitting room, an office for the ambassador's spouse, or as a small dining room, which is how it is used today. It is a room of beautiful proportions, with bright natural light streaming in from south-facing windows. With the Residence in constant demand, sometimes three breakfasts must be laid on simultaneously: this room invariably hosts one of them.

Lutyens places the fireplace angled across a corner of the room with a mirror above, a popular device of his. This room has a window which appears to be facing outdoors, but in fact overlooks the staircase well, allowing the curious to spy on guests arriving and leaving the Residence. Middleton Park (Oxfordshire, 1938) was similarly designed with a small window in a bedroom so that the children could peer down and see what was happening below.

ABOVE Lutyens' trick window, which looks down over and through the Grand Staircase to a stone urn atop a niche in the Old Chancery façade, with a window seat from which the curious can spy.

FACING PAGE The table in the Morning Room expands to allow for up to twelve to sit in comfort.

Ballroom

Diplomacy can involve an element of theatre. The question is, what play are you putting on?
And the great thing about the Residence is that it's infinitely adaptable.

Sir David Manning, British Ambassador to the United States, 2003–7

The Ballroom, the largest room in the house, is almost square. Lutyens designed an uncluttered room that has allowed for multiple uses over the decades. It has been a drawing room, a reception hall, a lecture theatre and a space for state and other grand dinners, allowing many more guests to be entertained in style than in the main Dining Room.

The room has no entrance doors, and flows directly out of the Main Corridor, the separation defined by a row of four elegant columns, similar to those employed by Lutyens in the hall at Heathcote (West Yorkshire, 1906). The casual observer would conclude these columns were constructed of the finest Siena marble, but in fact they are metal covered with scagliola, a composite substance imitating marble used extensively in great eighteenth-century British houses. The same colouring and materials are used for the two fireplace surrounds here in the Ballroom (and in the Dining Room and Drawing Room), complemented with real white marble.

At the far end of the room are three full-length terraced windows which lead out to an inner courtyard. In between them are hung full length mirrors, comprising regular pieces of smoky mirror, a common device in houses of the 1920s. Mirrors are placed also on either side of the artificial pillars by the fireplaces. As with the eighteenth-century architect John Soane, Lutyens deployed mirrors to play with light and reflection, and to magnify the size of his rooms. Lutyens was much aggrieved at being told to reduce the size of the Ballroom: 'he would have loved to have had another six feet each way', commented Allan Greenberg.[7] He was particularly upset to lose height, so the mirrors were partly meant to counteract that lack of vertical space.

The small courtyard beyond the windows at the north end is one of the house's many delights and guests can flow out into it. Similarly, through the pillars, lies the Portico. Large receptions, when the weather permits, can thus see guests spread outdoors at either end of the Ballroom.

Elaborately carved floral friezes run around the entire room, and the patterns continue into the Main Corridor, helping to create the sense of one unified space. They are directly inspired by the work of Grinling Gibbons, the seventeenth-century English master woodcarver. The room is dominated by three heavy chandeliers, said to have been brought from the former Embassy in Connecticut Avenue, along with the Persian Tabriz carpet of quite exceptional quality. Ever the master of detail, the electric-light fittings were all made in London by Messrs Higgins and Cattle, and set out to Lutyen's precise instructions. His rooms often leave little space for hanging pictures. The Andy Warhol portrait of Queen Elizabeth II fills one rare space, over the fireplace on the western wall.

FACING PAGE Lutyens had a deep understanding of Classical architecture, and took great care with his designs, down to the minutest detail, as can be seen in these Corinthian capitals above the faux marble pillars that outline the Ballroom. Lutyens' original plan for the Ballroom and the rest of the house called for a carved marble frieze and marble pilasters, floors, columns and fireplace surrounds. The contract was soon amended at the Treasury's behest to make savings: the frieze and pilasters were to be changed to plaster, black marble tiles on the floor to slate and the columns and fireplace surrounds to scagliola.

PAGES 140–1 The Ballroom from the Main Corridor facing northwards in the direction of the Inner Courtyard. The two mirrors on each side and at the end make the room appear larger. This is the room where Lutyens most regretted the economies forced on him by the Treasury.

ABOVE, TOP A sculpture on the frieze, with local plants portrayed below. Lutyens was fond of using local flora in his designs.

ABOVE, BOTTOM A putto of a chubby male child adorned with local flowers.

FACING PAGE A view of the Ballroom looking southwards across the Main Corridor, through the Portico outside the door and into the Garden. The three doors and two mirrors on this south side offer a perfect echo of those on the north side.

Andy Warhol (1928–87)

Queen Elizabeth II of the United Kingdom, 1985
Screenprint with diamond dust on board

Andy Warhol's iconic image of Queen Elizabeth II hovers between the formality of a traditional portrait and the brashness of modern advertising. Blocks of colour are slightly misaligned, recreating the immediacy of mass-produced commercial images. Each contour is sprinkled with diamond dust, in playful acknowledgment of the sitter's royalty.

Warhol was fascinated by the idea of reproducing familiar images. From portraits of Marilyn Monroe to Coca Cola bottles, he appropriated commercial images as the basis for his works. This portrait was based on the official 1977 Jubilee portrait photograph of The Queen – an internationally recognised image. Warhol's portrait is one of several portraits of Elizabeth II from his series, *Reigning Queens*, which included images of the Queens of Denmark and the Netherlands.

Andy Warhol, one of the most famous Pop Artists of the twentieth century, was born Andrew Warhola to Czechoslovakian parents in Pittsburgh. He studied painting and drawing at the Carnegie Institute of Technology in Pittsburgh between 1945 and 1949, before becoming a highly successful commercial advertising artist in the 1950s. The Pop Art he then developed was a reaction to Abstract Expressionism exemplified by the work of artists such as Jackson Pollock and Mark Rothko.

In the early 1960s, Warhol began painting his characteristic images of mass-produced consumer goods, notably Brillo Pads and Campbell's Soup tins. He later adopted screenprinting as his preferred medium; its smooth effacement of the artist's touch mirroring the faceless banality of contemporary consumerism. As his art developed during the 1960s, he fused images of popular culture, mass production, Hollywood glamour and the media with notions of what constituted 'fine art'. Despite announcing his retirement in the mid-1960s, Warhol continued to produce films and works of art while managing the rock band The Velvet Underground. The portrait featured here is a later work, made in 1985, shortly before he died in 1987. Hung over the fireplace, it catches the eye of every visitor to the Ballroom. Most can't believe that such a grand ambassadorial residence would give pride of place to such a bold contrast to the traditional portraits they might normally associate with members of the royal family. Almost everyone who addresses a reception or a dinner in the Ballroom does so under Her Majesty's colourful smile.

CHANTAL CONDRON, *UK Government Art Collection*

If the Ballroom was the most compromised of Lutyens' rooms in the Residence, he returned to form with the Dining Room and the Drawing Room. Lutyens kept the former relatively plain, with two large windows at the end facing west and three windows along the north side. A simple panelling is recessed around the fireplace, which has two recessed circles, a typical Lutyens feature. A large but narrow mantelpiece dominates the room. Two pillars were later placed at the east end of the room, and simple carved features run along the frieze at the top.

FACING PAGE In the middle of the Dining Room table is a large George III silver *surtout de table* in three sections, the sides mounted with four cast royal coats of arms. On it is placed a silver centrepiece comprising three musicians, inscribed on the underside 'British Embassy to Washington', all the work of the celebrated silversmith Paul Storr in 1815. On either side are a pair of George IV silver soup tureens and covers, applied with cast royal coats of arms to both sides, inscribed on the underside 'Her Majesty's Embassy at Washington', made by James Collins in 1827. The fireplace behind is in Classical style with pillars on either side, a common style in Lutyens' fireplaces, with a similar example at Midland Bank in Poultry, designed around the same time.

RIGHT Resting against the silver centerpiece is the menu for the return dinner at the Residence in honour of President and Mrs George H. W. Bush given by The Queen on the occasion of her state visit on 16 May 1991. All invitations and menus for state visits are printed by Buckingham Palace, which maintains the custom of presenting menus in French.

On the occasion of the State Visit to the United States of America
of Her Majesty Queen Elizabeth II
and His Royal Highness The Prince Philip, Duke of Edinburgh
the British Ambassador is commanded by The Queen to invite

to an Investiture to be held at the Ambassador's Residence
on Tuesday, 8th May, 2007 at 12.30 p.m.

In Confirmation   *Dress: Business Suit / Day Dress*

Guests are asked to arrive between 11.50 a.m. and Noon
Please bring the enclosed Entry Card with you

PAGES 148–9 Lutyens' beautifully proportioned room is shown in this photograph of the candles being lit for a capacity of thirty-four for dinner in the Dining Room.

ABOVE A lion rampant finial on a silver soup tureen.

RIGHT An invitation to an investiture at the Residence on the occasion of the state visit of The Queen on 8 May 2007.

FACING PAGE The Dining Room looking towards the west wall. An arresting portrait of an *Unknown Gentleman in a Green Velvet Cap* (circa 1740–5) by William Hogarth (1697–1764) possibly depicts one of the artist's friends.

The candelabra, cutlery and silver came from the British embassies at Lisbon and The Hague, and were sent to Washington in 1893 when the British legation first became a fully accredited Embassy. Much of the silver dates from the early nineteenth century; many pieces were designed by the famous silversmith Paul Storr, while the silver punch bowl was made by John Bertelot of London in 1752. Two principal dinner services are used on formal occasions. One is made by Minton in golden green, with a royal coat of arms, the design being called 'Guyatte'. The other set, marking the Commemoration banquet at Lancaster House in London on 5 June 1953, is a golden white set made by Wedgwood. This design is known as 'Golden Persephone' and bears the royal coat of arms and the initials ER, for Elizabeth Regina (queen), in gilt. The distinctive chairs were originally commissioned for the British Embassy in Rio de Janeiro.

Drawing Room

Lutyens liked his principal reception rooms to face southwards onto the gardens. The Drawing Room lies at the south-west corner of the Residence. He gives this room an ornate, gently tiered ceiling, in contrast to the plain coved ceiling in the Dining Room. To light the room, he designed three smaller chandeliers in place of the two large ones in the Dining Room.

In 1950, the architect A.S.G. Butler said of this room: 'there is great learning and much delicacy in the treatment of this apartment. The relation of the fireplace to the panelling could not be better.'[8]

Lutyens loved fireplaces and designing them in contrasting styles; at the Viceroy's House, they all are different. In contrast to the Residence's Dining Room, in the Drawing Room he has designed a simpler fireplace, in white marble, metal painted to look like marble and white painted wood, and more prominent pelmets. The mantel is unusually narrow, although some of his mantels elsewhere, such as at Middleton Park, are of similar proportions.

The Drawing Room is another of the Residence's principal delights. Lighter than the Dining Room, Lutyens designed a room for the ambassador and family to use domestically, as well as for official entertaining. In his early 'vernacular' phase, Lutyens often used small casement-style window panes. But in his later Classical designs, as in Washington, he employed Georgian sash windows, which let in more light than casements, while avoiding broad expanses of glass. The six large sash windows are the secret of the room's success, which offer generous views of the ever-changing gardens on two sides of the house.

RIGHT The view that greets visitors as they enter the Drawing Room, displaying two prominent south-facing windows on the left-hand side. **FACING PAGE** Afternoon tea set out on one of a pair of carved giltwood console tables in the manner of William Kent (1685–1748), that were made in the early twentieth century. The room features a pair of George II-style carved wall mirrors, which reflect views of the garden opposite. **PAGES 154–5** A view of the Drawing Room looking in a westerly direction. The plain wooden floor harks back to Lutyens' early vernacular period. The fireplace is of a deliberately contrasting design to the fireplace in the Dining Room. The striking *Still Life* by the Scottish Colourist artist George Leslie Hunter (1877–1931) is a focal point at the end of the room.

Anteroom and Vestibule

At the east end of the Drawing Room is the Anteroom. At just nine feet by fourteen, it is ample for a meal or meeting for up to four people and has a single window to the east facing onto the Portico and to the south facing down to the gardens. Beautifully illuminated by natural light, and of striking height, Lutyens has designed a room whose presence is out of all proportion to its size.

Heading back eastwards towards the Ambassador's Study the visitor passes first the Ballroom on the left and then the Morning Room on the right. Immediately following this comes a very special part of the corridor. Using four columns, matching those in the Ballroom, Lutyens created a unique, symmetrical Vestibule providing, on one side, an alcove designed to showcase a work of art and, on the other, access to the Circular Staircase that leads to the upper floors.

RIGHT A view of the beautifully proportioned Anteroom from the Drawing Room looking eastwards across the Portico through the window. The barrel vault makes this room taller than it is wide.
FACING PAGE The Main Corridor features this circa 1730 George II carved giltwood console table in the rococo style, above which hangs *The Meeting or Have a Nice Day, Mr Hockney 1981–3* by Peter Blake (b. 1923). Oil on canvas, on loan from Tate Collection.

Circular Staircase

Lutyens was one of the most dramatic of architects, revelling in suspense, the unexpected, the stylish, the comic and in *panache*. In the Residence, he was able to make two major statements with staircases, the sweeping Grand Staircase at the entrance, and another much less commonly seen. This is the Circular Staircase, a style he loved to use, as at the now demolished private house he designed in London's Cheyne Walk. The Circular Staircase lies on the opposite side of the Main Corridor to the Morning Room, and takes visitors staying overnight to the bedroom floor above. It is the epitome of a Lutyens design, which he is said to have sketched initially with a calligraphy pen. Light filters down from above and is then cleverly picked up by the stairs, a design deliberately intended to encourage guests to move upwards. Both the Grand Staircase and the Circular Staircase are made entirely of limestone and share an interesting characteristic with many of his other staircases: the treads are both shorter in height and wider in depth than the norm, making the visitor almost glide forward. Lutyens took a particular delight in this stunning staircase, echoing the design elsewhere, which constituted the perfect marriage of function and aesthetics.

BELOW Silk banner of the royal arms, now mounted in a glazed giltwood frame. Formerly the property of William Duke of Clarence, later to become William IV.

FACING PAGE A circular form of fine, polished wood, Nigel Hall's sculpture *Intension Extension* (1995) echoes Lutyens' elegant balustrade and geometric floor pattern at the base of the Circular Staircase.

PAGES 160–1 This photograph reveals the full geometric masterpiece of Lutyens' spiral staircase design. He plays with the concept of spiral in the pattern of the support for the metal railings, creating a dazzling effect.

Secondary Rooms

Lutyens devoted the entire upper floor to bedrooms, arranged off one long corridor. He allowed for eight bedrooms, together with a boudoir and two dressing rooms. Since Acland's time as ambassador (1986–91), the bedrooms have been named after former ambassadors, starting with Howard, who laboured so long in the 1920s to make the new embassy a reality. Every ambassador until Dean is commemorated by either a bedroom or a sitting room. The grandest room, used by the most senior visitors, has a large en suite sitting room so that its occupants and their advisors can work in quiet.

RIGHT This green table, discovered a few years ago in storage, is believed to be an original Lutyens design. It is the only piece of Lutyens furniture in the Residence.

ABOVE The corridor landing on the bedroom floor. Here the designs are much simpler than on the corridor directly below and Lutyens allows much more space for hanging works of art.

RIGHT Detail of the balustrade on the upper landing leading to this pair of upper bedrooms. The design is the same as on the detail above the doorway to the garden, illustrated on page 18. The doors to the bedrooms can be seen in the background.

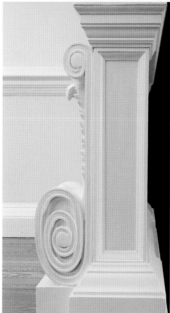

Portico

Lutyens had a focal point, a destination, in mind for all his buildings. At the Residence, it is this stunning portico. In almost fifty major houses he designed, he used a portico on only one other occasion, at Gledstone Hall. So it constitutes his most specific homage to *American* architecture, specifically to a traditional Virginia plantation house. Lutyens designed the frieze in particular as a deliberate salute to American Colonial craftsmen who were fond of this device for mantelpieces and ceiling cornices. This deep and broad space, dominated by thick Ionic columns arranged in rows of four and two, provides the most striking vista of the entire Residence.

As the land slopes away down towards the south, the Portico offers an ideal platform for the many speeches given over the years. The effect of the two columns behind the front four imparts depth, emphasising the long, shady porch so necessary in American houses. The paving slates in front of the Portico are of the same black-and-white colour that we see on the floor inside the Residence. The black is provided by the distinctive Lutyens feature of laying paving slates on their side tightly pressed together, giving the black squares a textured feel. Lutyens loved this device, and employed it also on the loggia at Gledstone Hall. Hundreds of thousands of shoes have trodden the surface, yet it still looks fresh and striking. Like many of the steps at the Residence, both inside and out, the steps leading down from the Portico into the garden are notably shallow. This is a feature seen commonly in Lutyens' work, such as at Marsh Court (Hampshire, 1904). In this case, the unexpected proportions play on the alternation between limestone and brick. The Portico, with its echoes of the White House, makes the Residence resemble the house of a leader of a great nation.

BELOW Lutyens' original drawing of the design of the Portico, with two pillars nearest the house and four pillars closest to the garden. The left-hand side depicts the floor, the right-hand the ceiling. The photograph opposite shows how the design translated into reality when the floor came to be laid out in stone and slate.

FACING PAGE In Lutyens' later buildings, it is common for the terrace leading onto the garden to be the focal point or highlight of his entire conception. This is the view from the Terrace, under the Portico, looking south towards the garden. In the 1930s, were Sir Ronald and Lady Lindsay to have eaten breakfast here, they would have been able to see the city centre in the distance.

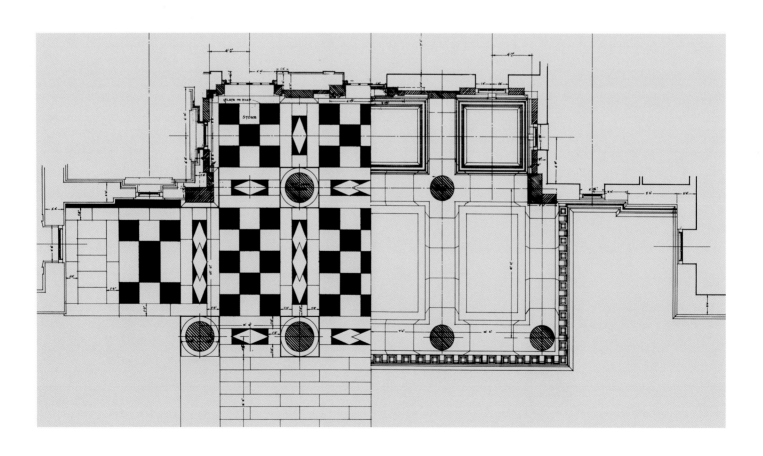

THE GARDEN

The History of the Garden

Lutyens' Concept of a Garden

PAGES 166-7 The perfect English garden, and the only one Lutyens designed in the United States. His love of blending built and natural environments, his use of walls, hedges, steps, and a range of levels, are all vividly on display here.
FACING PAGE A view of the Portico looking eastwards towards Massachusetts Avenue. Here can be seen the garden that Lutyens laid out, brushing right up to, and even clambering up onto, his Residence. The gingko trees on either side of the columns were recently planted to recreate the design of the 1930s, seen in the photographs of Churchill on pages 56-7 and page 71.
BELOW The diagram of the garden, with the north at the top. The prime place Lutyens gave to the rose gardens can be clearly seen, as can the pronounced east-west axis from the entrance on Massachusetts Avenue to the swimming pool on the far left.

Lutyens was far more than a designer of houses and their contents. He never visualised his buildings in isolation from their settings in the countryside of which they were a part. He wanted his houses to grow organically out of the land, constructed from local materials, worked on by craftsmen from the area, and he saw the gardens surrounding them as part of a unified whole. More than many architects, his was an integrated vision, with building and nature working in perfect harmony.

The plan shows the garden as it is today with the extra land adjacent to Massachusetts Avenue (acquired in 1931) below the Old Chancery building. Lutyens was able to exploit and enjoy the slopes in the land to great effect, as we see in the pages that follow.

Lutyens took great care to ensure his principal rooms offered generous views of the gardens. He conceived his gardens architecturally, with long garden walkways through them matching the long corridors he loved in his buildings. He wanted his gardens to feature differing and contrasting materials; to offer differing views, levels and spaces; and to dazzle visitors with colour. The various areas of his garden thus matched the rooms inside his buildings, emphasising the unity of vision of this extraordinary man. Garden 'walls' might be built from hedges or shrubs, or of brick and stone. In his gardens, we can perceive an ever-present sense of his keen intellect at work, as if we might encounter him around the next hedge.

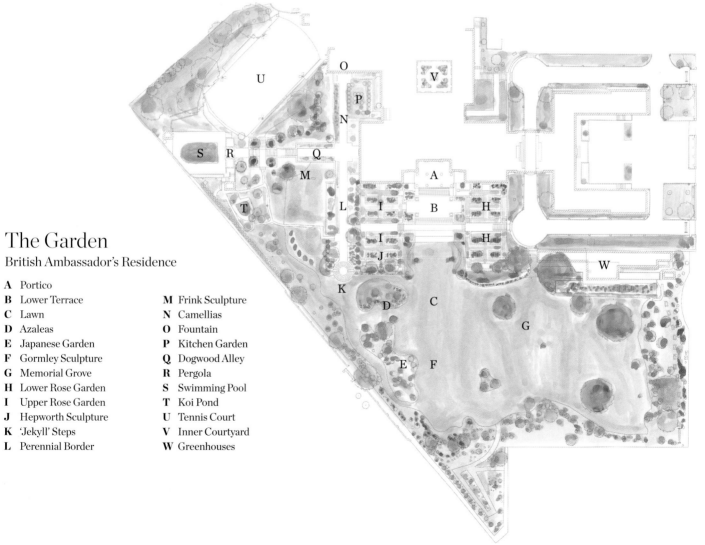

The Garden
British Ambassador's Residence

A Portico
B Lower Terrace
C Lawn
D Azaleas
E Japanese Garden
F Gormley Sculpture
G Memorial Grove
H Lower Rose Garden
I Upper Rose Garden
J Hepworth Sculpture
K 'Jekyll' Steps
L Perennial Border
M Frink Sculpture
N Camellias
O Fountain
P Kitchen Garden
Q Dogwood Alley
R Pergola
S Swimming Pool
T Koi Pond
U Tennis Court
V Inner Courtyard
W Greenhouses

Lutyens and Jekyll

Gertrude Jekyll was Lutyens' lifetime garden collaborator. When they first met, in the 1890s, Lutyens was a young architect barely embarked on his career, while the older Jekyll was already an experienced garden designer and horticulturalist. She was also a prodigious writer, producing over fifteen books and some thousand articles. She collaborated with Lutyens on a hundred or so of the more than four hundred gardens she created, many of which were photographed in *Country Life*, the publication that did so much to burnish both their reputations.

Although he knew little about plants, Lutyens shared with Jekyll a deep affection for the English countryside and for the use of traditional building materials, as well as an ability to visualise the spaces needed to showcase generous plantings. She helped him focus on the importance of features such as terraces, walkways and paving, which, deployed skilfully in garden design, would enhance the architectural elements of a building. Through his work with Jekyll, Lutyens began to see gardens as not just an optional add-on but fundamental to his concept of a perfect house. As he once put it: 'A garden scheme should have a backbone, a central idea beautifully phrased. Every wall, every path, stone and flower should have its relationship to the central idea.'[1]

As the twentieth century progressed, Lutyens' international fame grew and he and Jekyll worked together less often, although they remained friends until her death in 1932. While it is possible that Lutyens discussed the design of the Embassy garden with her, this was not a joint collaboration. Her influence, however, is unmistakable. In the Terrace, a central feature of many of their designs together, we feel her presence, as we do in the carefully designed paving. Many Lutyens-Jekyll gardens feature brick paving, with the bricks placed on their sides. Lutyens echoes this device in the Residence Terrace, eschewing bricks in favour of slate placed side by side. The ample space he created for the Perennial Border, an important element in Jekyll's gardens, is another reflection of her influence. A walk through the Residence Garden reminds us that for all Lutyens' genius, his experiences with Jekyll remained a significant intellectual repository, which he drew from freely in creating his own garden designs.

RIGHT The splendidly attired Gertrude Jekyll by a pond at her beloved Munstead Wood, designed by Lutyens in 1897. She was famed for her 'hardy flower borders', and for her stunning use of colour, which was compared to the work of the Impressionist painters who were working at the same time. She was originally a painter herself until her eyesight began to fail. Her most celebrated book is *Colour in the Flower Garden*.

FAR RIGHT The circular staircase at Folly Farm (1902). The similarity with the circular staircase Lutyens designed at the Residence twenty-five years later, facing page, is very marked. Notice the plants growing between the steps at Folly Farm, a favoured Jekyll device, blending natural and built environments.

FACING PAGE The distinctive circular staircase in the south-west corner of the garden. For an aerial view of the steps when first laid out, look at the black-and-white photograph on page 173. The steps are popular with guests today in part because they offer a distinctive echo for anyone standing in the centre.

Financing the Garden

Despite the brilliance of Lutyens' design for the Embassy garden, there was no guarantee that it would ever be realised. By 1930, the building itself had proved so expensive to construct that there was no money left for the garden to be laid out according to his careful plan. The prospect loomed of Lutyens' work being left unfinished. To the rescue came a British subject who was resident in New York, Samuel Agar Salvage, who had introduced rayon into the United States. Supported by eight other British subjects, he donated the sum of £10,000, sufficient to underwrite the cost of the garden, and to provide for the construction of a hard tennis court and swimming pool designed by Lutyens (an earlier plan for a temple as a focal point was abandoned). The names of the British benefactors are carved in stone at the entrance to the swimming pool.

A further boost was the surprising if welcome news of two adjacent plots for sale lying immediately to the south of the Chancery, affording a much longer frontage onto Massachusetts Avenue. Sir Ronald Lindsay, the ambassador, ascertained that the plot might be bought for only £32,000. In the feverish property market of Washington, he wrote to Lionel Earle in London: 'the first thing I want to impress on you is to keep your project secret. Don't tell anyone we are in the market; especially any American'.[2]

The financial climate had improved by the early 1930s and the British Treasury was willing to listen. The purchase would prevent unwelcome construction to the immediate south of the Embassy, detracting significantly from its aesthetics and its presence as a national emblem. The Treasury noted wryly, however, that had the purchase taken place some years earlier, the plot could have been obtained at a fraction of the cost. Mark Bertram, the historian of British embassies, noted an added irony that had this land been acquired in the 1920s, the whole site would have been a much more sensible shape and Lutyens would never have needed to come up with his elongated and clever design.[3] The Treasury, 'somewhat surprisingly' in Earle's words, agreed to the purchase. The newly purchased plot had been allowed to grow wild for years. It was not cultivated and made part of the garden until Lord Lothian, Lindsay's successor as ambassador in 1939, dug into his own pockets to provide the necessary funding.

RIGHT The word 'generosity' can be seen clearly carved above the entrance to the swimming pool. The full carving reads: 'This garden was laid out in the year 1930 by the generosity of eight British subjects resident in the U.S.A.'

ABOVE An aerial photograph of the gardens, 1931. The tennis court can be seen at the top left, as can the young red oaks planted on the lawn by Lady Lindsay, which have not survived. Her aim had been to create a forced perspective from the Portico down towards the views of the city centre. The layout of the sixteen principal rose beds can be clearly seen. In the bottom right foreground, note the scrubland, which constituted one of the two plots of land purchased in the early 1930s. Above the scrubland can be seen the driveway to the Residence: Massachusetts Avenue lies off the picture to the right.

Enter Lady Lindsay

The generosity of Samuel Salvage and his fellow funders had made it possible to create the bare bones of Lutyens' vision, but there was still much to do in establishing a living garden. Hundreds of flowers, plants and trees had to be selected and carefully planted within the framework to bring the design to life. Much of the burden fell to Lady Lindsay, the American wife of Sir Ronald Lindsay, the British ambassador from 1930.

The garden could not have had a better steward. Prior to her marriage in 1924, Elizabeth Sherman Hoyt, as she then was, had become a professional garden designer. In the early 1900s, 'garden design' was one of the few professions open to women. She duly studied at Radcliffe College, the women's college associated with Harvard College, and at its arboretum, graduating in 1910. She also befriended Beatrix Farrand, the *de facto* leader of the emerging women's landscape-gardening movement, who was herself influenced by the writings of Jekyll. As one of the eleven charter members (and the only woman) of the American Society of Landscape Architects, Farrand's credentials were beyond doubt. Sherman Hoyt worked at her office between 1910 and 1914 and learnt much from the experience.

Farrand was Edith Wharton's niece and the two were close. As Wharton lived and wrote about the 'Golden Age' in New York society, Farrand designed exquisite gardens for a clientele often not far removed from Wharton's literary creations. Her work included Bellefield, a walled garden in Hyde Park, New York, for Thomas Newbold, and the garden for the Morgan Library in New York. Most importantly for our purposes, she designed

Dumbarton Oaks in Washington, a 54-acre garden originally for Robert and Mildred Bliss. This estate lay less than a mile south of the new Embassy. Lady Lindsay was a long-standing friend of Mildred Bliss, and the two kept up a regular correspondence. Although there is little evidence that they corresponded specifically about the plans for the Embassy garden, Farrand's Dumbarton Oaks was an important influence on Lady Lindsay, who aspired to create a garden equally admired at 3100 Massachusetts Avenue.

Soon after taking up residence in June 1930, Lady Lindsay started to direct the planting. Two weeks after moving in she was writing feverishly on reorganising the lower garden and overseeing the planting of shrubs and trees. Progress was slow, but rewarding. 'I have gone native, and am having the time of my life', she wrote to a friend in late 1932. 'I have five men working in the garden and am out from 8am until 4pm every day, rather resentfully dashing in to entertain some infernal nuisance for lunch.'[4]

Her work rapidly began to bear fruit. The garden party, held in April 1933 for Prime Minister Ramsay MacDonald's second visit to the United States, received an enthusiastic write-up in the *The Washington Post*. Describing the Portico, under which the 1,100 guests were received, as 'overlooking one of the most beautiful panoramic views of the city', it went on to praise the new gardens as 'never more beautiful than in the bright spring sunshine of yesterday'.[5] That November, Lindsay wrote: 'no proud mother has ever been more moved at her child's first step than I am on seeing the oak trees, which we planted, put on their autumn coloring'.[6]

By June 1935, the garden bustled with 'fragrant roses planted in square and oblong plots about the grounds', while 'rare species of Iris or wax-like tulips nearby gave the effect of gay little mats on the velvety grass of the grounds'.[7] In the tradition of Jekyll, Lindsay took care with the colour patterns on her flower borders and was meticulous to avoid careless cutting of blooms. The garden now boasted red, white and mauve tulips in May, and, from June, roses that became famous across the city. It was said that an invitation to a reception at the British Embassy was second only to one at the White House. In no time at all, the new embassy and its remarkable new inhabitants had achieved the same cachet among Washington's elite as the old embassy on Connecticut Avenue.

The Garden from 1940

In June 1940, just after the fall of France to the Nazis, the new ambassador, Lord Lothian, hosted the first garden party at the Embassy for the general public. Up to 5,000 attended, enjoying to the full the new garden areas while raising money for 'Bundles for Britain', an American relief agency. His successor, Lord Halifax, continued this tradition of inviting the public to the gardens, and in June 1942 hosted one of many charity events, with visitors paying one dollar each to attend in aid of British War Relief. The following June saw the gardens used for the first time by an outside body, when the United Nations Club held its first anniversary celebration in the garden: the meetings that laid the groundwork for the United Nations itself were held at nearby Dumbarton Oaks.

The garden evolved gradually in the years that followed and today continues to delight and inspire visitors, as well as those who live and work at the Embassy. For all the changes that have occurred in the diplomatic scene since the 1930s, Lutyens' original conception of an English country garden continues to shine through.

FACING PAGE Early photograph of the swimming pool and the Residence behind. The view is unrecognisable today because of the subsequent growth of trees and plants (see page 199). Part of Lutyens' skill was to visualise how the built structures in his gardens would adapt to the growth of plants and trees all around them. ABOVE Lady Lindsay, the figure who let Lutyens' designs bloom, here standing in front of some Kwanzan cherry trees on 24 April 1939. Of the twenty-four cherry trees that she planted in the upper and lower Rose Gardens, only two now survive on each periphery. Another two flourish in the Perennial Border. They can be seen in their infancy in the aerial photo on page 173. PAGES 176-7 The view from the bedroom floor looking down under the Portico and over the Lower Terrace towards the lawns. Lutyens' design of gardens displays the same elegant sense of proportion and harmony as the interiors of his buildings.

THE GARDEN TOUR

View from the Portico towards the Lawn

BELOW On the left is the back of a Japanese maple planted by The Prince of Wales and The Duchess of Cornwall in 2005. The large tree in the background to the right is a maple planted by The Prince and Princess of Wales in 1985.
FACING PAGE The view from the Main Corridor looking under the Portico towards the Lawn, at the end of which is displayed *Extend*, a cast iron sculpture by Antony Gormley, 2011 (on loan from Antony Gormley, © Antony Gormley, Courtesy Sean Kelly, New York).

Lutyens designed the Portico and the view southwards to the gardens as the climax of his entire Embassy plan. In the 1930s, visitors would have been able to see the city skyline, including the Capitol and the Washington Monument, now obscured by the trees in the lower garden and in Rock Creek Park, some over a hundred feet tall. Visitors are invariably impressed by the generous expanse of lawn sweeping southwards. Their eye is also drawn from the Lower Terrace to the distinctive garden benches seen on pages 176–7, replicas in the Lutyens style. The uneven, rustic texture of Lutyens' slates, laid side to side, can be very clearly seen, a reminder of the enduring influence of the Arts and Crafts Movement. The gardens prove ideal for the display of sculpture by British artists, some permanent like *Single Form (Eikon)* by Barbara Hepworth and *Lying Down Horse* by Elisabeth Frink from the UK Government Art Collection, some temporary, like *Extend* by Antony Gormley.

FACING PAGE, TOP, LEFT The opposite side of the maple tree planted in 1985 by The Prince and Princess of Wales, looking back towards the house. The garden bench is a modern copy of Lutyens' original garden bench design, which can be seen also at Folly Farm on page 170.

FACING PAGE, TOP, RIGHT A glimpse of the back of *Lying Down Horse* by Elisabeth Frink against the backdrop of a grove of Japanese maples, showing their glorious colours in the autumn sunshine.

FACING PAGE, BOTTOM A view from the back of the garden towards the Residence. This is the most popular part of the Lawn for entertainment as guests spill out from the house and terraces to enjoy a stroll around the gardens.

ABOVE In the left foreground of the 'Memorial Grove' is the same maple as depicted in springtime on page 178, now shown resplendent in autumn.

Lawn

Visitors descend the steps onto the Lawn, which today regularly hosts a wide variety of events, including not only garden parties and other social events, but receptions showcasing the best of British products. The Residence gardens can be divided into the 'built' and the 'green' areas. Space for the latter was much extended when the extra land adjacent to Massachusetts Avenue was purchased in 1931, creating a far more generous expanse of lawn. Over the years, trees have been planted by visiting members of the royal family, spread over an area constituting a 'Memorial Grove'. The Residence garden now boasts seven of these 'royal trees', planted by three generations of the royal family: The Queen, The Prince of Wales and, most recently, Prince Harry.

Despite his liking for structures in gardens, Lutyens usually eschewed greenhouses. This can be understood in part as a reaction against Victorian fussiness and ornate glass buildings and by the preference of the Arts and Crafts Movement for simplicity and nature. Thus the greenhouses on the north east side of the Lawn were erected long after Lutyens' work was complete.

Rose Garden

Lutyens placed the 'upper' and 'lower' rose gardens to the left and right of the Portico and Lower Terrace. These rectangular rose gardens, in four sets of four, were to be the climax of his original concept and design. They are planted today with hybrid tea roses, a close copy of the roses that would have been bedded when the gardens were initially laid out. Gardening staff at the Residence have taken immense trouble to understand Lutyens' original designs. Studying early photographs, they have tried to replicate the original garden as closely as possible. The Rose Garden is bordered by Kwanzan cherry trees, which were planted and blooming when George VI visited the Residence in 1939.

The rose beds are all bordered in stone, the upper and lower gardens being contained within retaining brick walls. Lutyens' liberal use of built elements in his gardens is again on display, revealing his love of blending brick and stone, delineating different areas, and providing ideal spaces for the natural and built environment to meet. Climbing roses were one of his and Jekyll's hallmarks, and the device is used to great effect at the Embassy.

FACING PAGE Lutyens wanted his houses to look almost as if they had emerged from the ground, using stone, brick and other materials from the locality. He wanted his buildings to blend harmoniously with the gardens, as can be seen in this photograph of a corner of the lower Rose Garden, with the Ambassador's Study under the pediment and crest in the middle background.

RIGHT Lutyens took a particular joy in designing furniture for gardens as well as houses. One of the most common designs is this scrolled-back garden seat which can be seen in the upper Rose Garden against the wall of the Drawing Room. Similar replica benches are to be found in the garden of Number 10, Downing Street in London. The Zephirine Drouhin rose is an old Bourbon rose from 1868. One of the best known climbers in the world, this prolific and fragrant rose is the first to bloom in the spring.

The layout of the rose gardens illustrates how Lutyens turned the various slopes on the property to his advantage. The introduction of different gardens on different levels helps create the illusion of 'rooms' within the garden, an effect Lutyens prized. As ever, he sought to blend his gardens with his architecture and have each reflect the other. A perfectly flat site would have made it easier for him to create the Embassy buildings, but it might have made for a less enriching Residence and garden design.

The upper Rose Garden lies on the west side of the house. Here one finds the celebrated Barbara Hepworth sculpture *Single Form (Eikon)*. The gardens contain many of Lutyens' staple garden features – differing levels, sunken areas and ubiquitous walls, for example – but they lack ponds or channels of water: fishing was Lutyens' one outdoor pursuit and he revelled in using water whenever he could.

PAGES 184–5 This photo is taken along the garden axis from the west looking east, from the walkway in the upper Rose Garden. On the right are two large, round yews planted by Lady Lindsay. The two urns on the wall are part of Lutyens' original design and are repeated at the Chancery gates and elsewhere. The urns in the foreground and the fountain are later additions.

LEFT This is a detail of the lower Rose Garden, which can be seen in the left-hand corner of page 182. The rose is a hybrid tea rose entitled Queen Elizabeth II introduced in 1954. The winner of numerous awards, it is a favourite among rose breeders across the world. Notice the elaborate detailed work in the blend of stone and brickwork, the dramatic size of the keystone and the vista that is afforded of the wall in the distance through the aperture.

FACING PAGE This photo is taken from the roof, showing part of the Lower Terrace plus the upper Rose Garden to the right of the house, clearly illustrating the impact of geometry on Lutyens. The lines and squares make up complex geometric patterns, yet the grass, stone, slates, flowerbeds and shrubs all fuse together into a harmonious whole.

Single Form (Eikon) 1937–8, cast 1963
Bronze

Sited in a prominent position in the Residence Garden and seen from the south-facing windows of the Residence is a striking bronze sculpture by Barbara Hepworth, *Single Form (Eikon)*. Sent to Washington the same year it was purchased, 1965, the Embassy was selected as a suitably important location for a work by this internationally-acclaimed British artist. A bronze triangular shaft with a triangular top plane, the sculpture is one of seven bronze casts that Hepworth made in 1963 after an earlier plaster sculpture, *Single Form* (1937–8) that was exhibited in Paris until 1961.

Eikon is a Greek word with the broad definition of 'image' – a word that Hepworth added to the subtitle in 1963 to underpin what she regarded as the sculpture's figurative nature. In 1938, amid an increasingly charged political climate in Europe, her abstract work was criticised for being escapist. This observation was also based partly on Hepworth's membership of Abstraction-Création, an international artists' society based in Paris which favoured non-representational work. In her defence, Hepworth stated that her artistic approach was to explore humankind's relationship to the earth and its sensibility to the universe. A work such as *Single Form (Eikon)* symbolises man's contribution to landscape, echoing the ancient functions of Neolithic stone circles, as famously represented at Stonehenge and Avebury in England.

One of the leading sculptors of her time, Barbara Hepworth's work can be seen throughout the world. Born in Wakefield, Yorkshire, she studied at Leeds School of Art and the Royal College of Art. In 1924, she was awarded a scholarship in Italy to study marble carving. In 1932, she visited the Paris studios of leading French artists with fellow British artist, Ben Nicholson, whom she later married. At the forefront of the modern movement in England, Hepworth and Nicholson were members of influential artistic groups including the 7 and 5 Society and Unit One in London and Abstraction-Création in Paris.

At the outbreak of the Second World War, Hepworth, Nicholson and their triplets moved to Cornwall. After the end of their marriage in 1951, Hepworth remained in Cornwall, living and working in the peaceful surroundings of Trewyn Studios in St Ives. She was awarded a CBE in 1958 and a DBE in 1965. Hepworth died in 1975 following a fire in her studio. The Hepworth Museum and Sculpture Garden was opened in 1976 and today her studio is open to the public.

CHANTAL CONDRON, *UK Government Art Collection*

Perennial Border

A perennial border was a standard feature in many English gardens. In the Residence garden, Lutyens has two long vistas, both of which are clearly seen on the diagram on page 169 and the aerial photograph on page 173. The long line to the south of the house crosses the Perennial Border at right angles. The circular steps, otherwise known as the 'Jekyll steps', mark the lawn end of this border. The beds along the 100-foot walkway are some 15 feet deep on either side and are full of lush colours. Lady Sheinwald worked with the gardeners to restore authenticity to these beds during the time her husband, Sir Nigel Sheinwald, was ambassador from 2007 to 2012. Research was conducted into Jekyll's planting schemes as a source of inspiration and, as far as possible, the borders of today draw on her favoured plants and palette of colours. The Elisabeth Frink sculpture can be glimpsed over the Border on the lawns beyond.

Continuing in a northerly direction, the camellia bed is on the left, planted with ten different kinds of the plant along the brick wall. The kitchen garden sits at the north end, offering a combination of early spring and autumn plants, with a herb garden. Because of its location, in the shadow of the house, it is a difficult area to plant, but lettuces and cabbages thrive in the spring and autumn. At the end of the walkway, there are niches of neoclassical design. They were intended to be kept empty, but at some point, a fountain was installed inside one. Lutyens would not have approved!

PAGES 190–1 This is a view taken from the centre of the walkway that bisects the entire Rose Garden, taken at the bottom of the Lower Terrace. We see through the upper Rose Garden to the *heuchera* growing through the steps leading to the Perennial Border. The Hepworth sculpture is to the left, obscured from view by one of Lady Lindsay's yews in the left foreground. The carefully manicured lawn in the foreground, along with the tightly-clipped hedges, contrast with the more free-flowing trees and shrubs of the background, creating a dramatic effect of retreating civilisation.

RIGHT The focal point of the Perennial Border is the curved recess in the shape of a domed doorway. The subsequent insertion of the fountain compromises the effect that one might be re-entering a building at the end of the pathway.

FACING PAGE Viewed across the Perennial Border as well as from the west-facing windows in the Drawing Room, Elisabeth Frink's sculpture *Lying Down Horse* is always a favourite with visitors to the Residence Garden, especially children.

PAGES 194–5 The Perennial Border is a delight throughout the year with a constantly changing palette of colours and shapes. The path runs north-south, passing the elaborate entrance in stone on the west side of the house. In front, to the right of the entrance, lies the Drawing Room, deliberately placed by Lutyens to afford maximum views of the gardens to the front and side.

Cymbidium

The *Cymbidium* orchid was first named in 1799, taking its title from the Greek word *kymbos,* 'a boat-shaped cup', referring to the sculpted shape of some of the flower lips. There are fifty-two evergreen species of this orchid.

Cymbidiums are cool-growing orchids which flower at high altitudes. Generally larger plants with waxy blooms, they are terrestrial and live unusually long lives. They flourish in East Asia, and are found in India, Japan, Malaysia, the Philippines, Borneo and Northern Australia. In China, this orchid type is much beloved by local painters, as they are by artists in Japan. In some Malay villages, they were attributed mythical protective powers, with their roots used to cure sick elephants. In Bhutan, certain Cymbidiums are considered a culinary delicacy and are used to flavour curry or stew.

Tropical orchids were first imported to Britain in 1731, and by 1783 thirteen exotic species were being grown at the royal gardens in Kew, to the delight of the royal family. But the arrival of cool-growing orchids was not far behind. Cymbidiums too have a long and storied association with Britain, where due to the thriving orchid trade of the nineteenth century many of the original species were first brought from Asia. A species is a wild, naturally occurring plant with usually little or no difference between individuals, called clones. *Cymbidium tracyanum*, illustrated on page 217, is one such example of a species, reflected by the fact that it has only one Latin name after *Cymbidium* – hybrids get a subsequent name, usually not in Latin. Named for H. A. Tracy, a prominent nineteenth-century British orchid grower and member of the RHS – like Sir George Holford and many other early orchid collectors and growers – *tracyanum* was awarded a First Class Certificate by the RHS in 1890.

Another species orchid, *Cymbidium lowianum*, named after the Scottish nurseryman, Hugh Low, is very important in the history of orchid hybridising. Responsible for the start of long breeding lines of modern-day upright Cymbidiums, it is an ancestor of *Cymbidium* Alexanderi 'Purity' and *Cymbidium* Alexanderi 'Westonbirt', among many others. *Cymbidium lowianum* 'Concolor', illustrated on page 217, is a naturally occurring variant of *lowianum*.

Cymbidiums normally bloom from late December and can remain in flower till May. Dependent on precise greenhouse conditions to prosper, they take five or more years from ripened seed to bloom. Colours range from white to pink and red, with some varieties offering yellow, green and brown blooms: some can even be black – but this orchid is never blue. Cymbidiums are one of the most popular of all orchids across the world on account of the beauty of their blooms, which can remain open for up to ten weeks. Each plant can produce fifteen or more flowers on each spike – one of their great attractions being that they can survive in cold temperatures. They were first imported into the United States from Britain in 1910 by Henry E. Huntington for his gardens in Santa Barbara, California, where the climate was particularly well suited for orchid growing.

FACING PAGE *Cymbidium* Phar Lap 'Aqua Caliente'.

ABOVE *Cymbidium* Burgundian 'Chateaux' FCC/RHS.

FACING PAGE (CLOCKWISE FROM TOP, LEFT) *Cymbidium tracyanum* FCC/RHS; *Cymbidium lowianum*
'Concolor' FCC/RHS; *Cymbidium* Volcanic Flash 'Tim Tom'.

Cattleya

Cattleyas were the most sought after orchids in Britain and the United States in the nineteenth century, when they became an essential fashion item for women on both sides of the Atlantic, who wore them in specially made vases that attached to button holes or lapels. Celebrated for their intoxicating fragrance and dazzling appearance, they were later proclaimed the 'Queen of Flowers'. In the twentieth century, women continued to wear them pinned to the bodice of their clothes as well as on their wrists as corsages, a style which remained immensely popular until the 1960s. Images of Cattleyas had meanwhile been used for decades to sell everything from gourmet food to liquor, and were commonplace on cigar boxes and china plates.

Cattleyas were named in 1824 by the eminent botanist John Lindley (1799–1865) in honour of Sir William Cattley (1788–1835), who was among the first to grow a specimen, *Cattleya labiata*, in Britain. One of the finest of all orchids, it arrived in England from Brazil as packing material around other plants thought to be of greater interest. Lindley's descriptions of it encouraged competition among growers to match or even surpass this magnificent plant. In 1857, the Royal Horticultural Society officially recognised a *Cattleya* cross as the first tropical hybrid. Britain remained a world leader in hybridising through the rest of the nineteenth century. Frederick Sander, known as the 'Orchid King', was thought to have around two million orchids at his nurseries in 1894. The first to realise that records needed to be kept of these new hybrids, in 1901 he started an orchid register, which eventually became known as *Sander's List of Orchid Hybrids*. In the 1960s, the RHS took over the registration of new hybrids, a role it maintains to this day. Thanks to the Sander family, it is possible to trace the full lineage of almost any orchid registered from 1856 to today.

Guarianthe skinneri 'Casa Luna', illustrated opposite, is a selection of the renowned *Cattleya skinneri* from Central America. A Scottish trader based in Guatemala, George Ure Skinner was an early plant collector and exporter who introduced almost one hundred new orchid species into cultivation in Britain for over thirty years from 1834. He sent orchids to Kew Gardens as well as to prominent collectors such as the Duke of Bedford. In the 1840s and 1850s, many of his orchids were sold at auctions in London.

The spread of orchid mania in the nineteenth century brought both plants and orchid growers across the Atlantic. Oliver Lines, a young nurseryman who worked for H. G. Alexander at Westonbirt, showed an aptitude for orchid growing from an early age. Interest in spectacular Cattleyas was enhanced in the United States after he emigrated in 1910 and found himself in high demand by owners of prestigious estates across the Eastern Seaboard who sought his expertise in growing their own Cattleyas. In the 1940s, he began a commercial venture in Tennessee. Among the orchids he bred from British stock is *Rhyncholaeliocattleya* Henrietta Japhet 'Lines', illustrated on page 221.

Traditionally difficult to grow, and needing a full five years from seed to bloom, Cattleyas were for a long time an exclusive orchid, but advances in technology have made their cultivation easier. New hybrid types will now bloom throughout the year, as opposed to during the traditional September to May period. The Residence collection includes significant holdings of renowned nineteenth-century Cattleyas, in addition to the best American hybrids of recent years.

FACING PAGE *Guarianthe skinneri* 'Casa Luna' AM/AOS.

ABOVE (CLOCKWISE FROM TOP, LEFT) *Cattleya* Junto 'Bright Eyes'; *Ryncholaeliocattleya* Goldenzelle
'Lemon Chiffon' AM/AOS; *Cattleya* Irene Finney 'York' AM/AOS.

FACING PAGE (CLOCKWISE FROM TOP, LEFT) *Rhyncholaeliocattleya* Henrietta Japhet 'Lines' AM/AOS;
Rhyncholaeliocattleya Fairfield; *Cattleya* Chia Lin 'New City' AM/AOS.

Oncidium

Athird principal group of orchids, *Oncidium*, takes its name from the Greek word *onkos,* meaning 'a tumour' or 'fleshy body', a reference to the warty growths on the floral lips of some species. First described by Olaf Swartz, a Swedish botanist, in 1800, *Oncidium* is a highly diverse genus of some five hundred and twenty species growing in the American tropics and subtropics, occurring in a wide variety of sizes from tiny plants of only a few centimetres to enormous plants with multiple branches which produce hundreds of flowers. Often slight and brightly coloured, they are famed for having petals which encircle a large lip. *Oncidium, Brassia, Bratonia, Oncostele* and *Psychopsis* are some of the numerous related genera that make up the *Odontoglossum* alliance. Many species originally classified as Odontoglossums and Oncidiums have subsequently been reclassified into genera of their own, leading to frequent – and confusing – name changes.

Considerable interest was sparked and orchid mania began in earnest after 1825, when Ralph Woodford (1784–1828) managed to bring an *Oncidium papilio* to England from Trinidad, where he had been governor. With the acquisition of *Oncidium papilio*, the 6th Duke of Devonshire, later President of the Royal Horticultural Society, embarked on creating at Chatsworth the most extensive collection of orchids at any private estate in Britain. Ably assisted by his gardener Joseph Paxton (1803–65), the most celebrated gardener of the Victorian era, he built three greenhouses to accommodate the collection, one of which is still standing.

Another orchid that played a major part in orchid mania, *Odontoglossum crispum* (now known as *Oncidium alexandrae*), originated in the Andes. Over two thousand clones of this species were named, with some so prized that 1150 guineas was paid for a single plant in 1906. It is at the base of the pedigree of both *Oncostele* Hot Pants 'Hot to Trot', illustrated on page 224, and *Oncostele* Catatante 'Pacific Sun Spots', illustrated on page 225.

Early growers referred to Odontoglossums as the 'Queen of Flowers' due to their dainty, lady-like blooms. The flowers display an unusually bright palette. Predominantly vivid golden yellow, they also come in soft autumnal colours. Their relative lack of fragrance is compensated by their comparative ease of growth with the flowers being in bloom from May through to August.

The Residence collection contains several unusual examples of this group of species, including *Brassia* Rex 'Lea', illustrated opposite, which can produce eighteen to twenty individual flowers, and is a most spectacular orchid when in full flower. The Collection also contains several inter-generic *Brassidium* (*Brassia x Oncidium*) crosses, with spikes of spider-like flowers of almost three feet. One such plant is *Brassia* Datacosa 'Coos Bay', illustrated on page 224.

Although many attractive hybrids such as *Oncostele* Catatante 'Pacific Sun Spots' are mass produced for the retail market, very few of the species remain abundant in the wild, due to the wanton over-collecting that characterised many pioneering 'orchid hunters' of the nineteenth century.

❖

FACING PAGE *Brassia* Rex 'Lea' AM/AOS.

FACING PAGE (CLOCKWISE FROM TOP, LEFT) *Bratonia* Olmec 'Kano' HCC/AOS; *Oncostele*
Hot Pants 'Hot to Trot'; *Brassia* Datacosa 'Coos Bay' AM/AOS.
ABOVE (CLOCKWISE FROM TOP, LEFT) *Oncostele* Catatante 'Pacific Sunspots'; *Psychopsis*
Memoria Bill Carter; *Oncidium* Macmex 'Orchidheights'.

Other Orchids

While a number of orchids in the Residence's collection, such as *Cymbidium* and *Cattleya*, have historic connections to Britain, other orchids are collected and displayed because of their particular beauty or the longevity of their blooms.

Prominent among these other species are *Phalaenopsis* orchids, renowned for their magnificent floral displays and ability to flourish without much light. Native to the tropical regions of the Indian Ocean, Borneo, the Philippines and Australia, *Phalaenopsis* are remarkably long-lived, with some remaining in bloom for several months. Modern technology has managed to reduce the time from seed to bloom to just eighteen months, explaining the phenomenal surge in the popularity of *Phalaenopsis* since the late twentieth century. They are now the popular orchid of choice, grown in Asia in vast quantities both as a plant and for the cut flower industry. A display of cut *Phalaenopsis* is today considered more exotic and certainly more enduring than a comparably priced floral arrangement or potted flowering plant.

Phalaenopsis are often found at the Residence, as hybridisation has allowed the traditional palette of white and pink to broaden out across a broader range of colours. A multi-coloured variety, *Phalaenopsis* Gan Lin Black Diamond, is illustrated on page 228.

In sharp contrast to the comparatively quick growing *Phalaenopsis*, 'slipper orchids' can take ten to twelve years from seed to bloom. Their distinctive characteristic is a pouch or slipper-shaped lip, which is a modification of the third petal of the orchid. *Paphiopedilum* is the most commonly grown of the four main genera of slipper orchids, and derives its name from the Greek word *pedilum*, meaning 'slipper' or 'sandal'. Early hybrids of this flower were large and almost round, primarily in shades of browns and greens. But in the latter twentieth century, yellow and pink flowered species from South East Asia and China became available. *Phragmipedium* is another popular slipper orchid, found mainly in Central and South America. Among slipper orchids that the Collection holds are *Phragmipedium* Fireworks 'April Fool' and *Paphiopedilum Keyeshill*, a relative of the very popular *Paphiopedilum* Winston Churchill, registered with the RHS in 1951, both illustrated on page 228.

Other orchids from the Residence collection include the wonderful white flowering *Maxillaria splendens* 'Lady Julia', illustrated on page 229, which is noted for its pleasing fragrance and its ability to flourish in those areas of the Residence with less natural light, a quality shared with *Ludisia discolor* 'Black Jewel', illustrated on page 209, referred to often as the coffee-table orchid. The Residence is also rich in orchids of the *Vanda* type, characterised by a flamboyant array of colours, such as *Vanda* Sansai Blue, illustrated opposite. Difficult to cultivate outside specialist nurseries, Vandas can grow as high as three feet, with blooms mainly in the spring and autumn.

❖❖❖

FACING PAGE *Vanda* Sansai Blue.

ABOVE (CLOCKWISE FROM TOP, LEFT) *Phalaenopsis* Gan Lin Black Diamond; *Phragmipedium* Fireworks 'April Fool' AM/AOS; *Paphiopedilum Keyeshill.*
FACING PAGE (CLOCKWISE FROM TOP, LEFT) *Dendrobium spectabile*; *Catasetum* Jumbo Eagle; *Maxillaria splendens* 'Lady Julia' AM/CCM/AOS.

Notes

■ 'The Finest Embassy in the World' (notes to pp. 19–23)
1. *Washington Post*, 22 December 1929.
■ Part I (notes to pp. 26–32)
1. David Reynolds, 'Prime ministers and presidents: special relationships' (lecture, 1 July 2012, 10 Downing Street).
2. Harold Nicolson, *The Spectator*, 22 December 1948.
3. Bryce to McDonnell, 28 November 1908, National Archives, Kew, UK, WORK 10/58.
4. Spring-Rice to Earle, 18 May 1913, WORK 10/58.
5. Earle to Spring-Rice, 16 April 1914, WORK 10/58.
6. Reynolds, 'Prime ministers and presidents'.
7. Craigie memo, 12 November 1928, cited in Kathleen Burk, *Old World, New World* (London: Little, Brown, 2007), p. 471.
8. Howard to Earle, 9 May 1924, WORK 10/58.
9. Henry Colyton, *Occasion, Chance and Change* (Wilby: Michael Russell, 1993), p. 53.
■ Part II (notes to pp. 36–54)
1. Wardman to Howard, 19 May 1924, National Archives, Kew, UK, WORK 10/100.
2. Gavin Stamp and Allan Greenberg, 'Modern architecture as a very complex art', in *Lutyens Abroad: The Work of Sir Edward Lutyens Outside the British Isles*, ed. Andrew Hopkins and Gavin Stamp (London: British School at Rome at the British Academy, 2002), p. 131.
3. Stamp and Greenberg, 'Modern architecture', p. 131.
4. Gavin Stamp, *Edwin Lutyens Country Houses: From the Archives of Country Life* (London: Aurum Press, 2012), p. 11.
5. Quoted in Tim Skelton and Gerald Gliddon, Lutyens and the Great War, Frances Lincoln, 2008, p. 25.
6. Earle to Howard, 15 May 1925, National Archives, WORK 10/100.
7. Ibid.
8. Earle to Lutyens, 22 June 1925, WORK 10/100.
9. Lutyens to Howard, 8 July 1925, WORK 10/100.
10. Barstow to Earle, 4 June 1925, cited in Stamp and Greenberg, pp. 134–5.
11. Lutyens to Earle, 7 March 1927, WORK 10/101.
12. Edwin Lutyens to Emily Lutyens, 15 February 1927, RIBA Archives, LuE 19/7/6.
13. Earle to Lutyens, 9 February 1927, WORK 10/101.
14. Wardman to Lutyens, 18 August 1930, WORK 57/2.
15. Lindsay to Earle, 20 October 1930, WORK 10/104.
16. Howard to Earle, 7 November 1928, WORK 10/103.
17. Howard to Earle, 20 June 1929, WORK 10/103.
18. Howard to Earle, 26 December 1929, WORK 10/103.
19. Howard to Earle, 30 September 1927, WORK 10/102.
20. Lindsay to Earle, 12 April 1930, WORK 10/103.
21. Edwin Lutyens to Emily Lutyens, 27 May 1930, RIBA Archives, LuE 19/15/4.
22. Lindsay to Earle, 2 June 1930, WORK 10/103.
23. Lady Lindsay to Lutyens, 20 June 1930, WORK 10/104.
24. Embassy diary, WORK 10/104.
25. Minute sheet, Office of Works, 2 February 1930, WORK 10/104.
26. Lady Lindsay to Earle, 14 March 1931, WORK 10/104.
27. Lady Lindsay to Lutyens, 14 March 1931, WORK 10/104.
■ Part III (notes to pp. 58–105)
At War: Forging the 'Special Relationship', 1939–45 (notes to pp. 68–78)
1. Lindsay to Halifax, 10 March 1939, National Archives, Kew, UK, FO 800/324.
2. Ibid.
3. Lothian to Halifax, 5 September 1939, FO 800/324.
4. Lothian to Halifax, 11 March 1940, Churchill Papers, Churchill College, Cambridge, CHAR 20/15/1.
5. Smith to Welles, 29 September 1940, NARA, College Park, MD, RG 59, Central Decimal File 1940–44, Box 1830.
6. Ian Kershaw, *Fateful Choices* (London: Allen Lane, 2007), p. 222.
7. Telegram #3057, 12 December 1940, National Archives, Kew, UK, FO 794/18.
8. Churchill to Roosevelt, 8 December 1940, Churchill College, Cambridge, UK, Churchill Papers, CHAR 23/4/11.
9. Halifax to Churchill, 10 April 1941, National Archives, PREM 4/27/9.
10. Roberts, *The Holy Fox*, p. 282.
11. Halifax to Churchill, 9 December 1941, National Archives, PREM 4/27/9.
12. Undated telegram, cited in Martin Gilbert, *Churchill and America* (New York: Free Press, 2005), p. 252.
13. Halifax to Churchill, 11 January 1942, National Archives, PREM 4/27/9.
14. Bevin to Attlee, 14 December 1946, National Archives, FO 800/513.
15. Frances Perkins, *The Roosevelt I Knew* (New York: Viking Press, 1946) p. 84.
16. Cited in David Dimbleby and David Reynolds, *An Ocean Apart: The Relationship between Britain and America in the Twentieth Century* (New York: Random House, 1988), p. 170.
17. Churchill to Roosevelt, 18 March 1945, Churchill Papers, CHAR 20/199.
Visit of George VI (pp. 61–5)
a. Halifax to Chamberlain, 16 November 1938, National Archives, Kew, UK, FO 794/17.
b. Note by Lindsay, 6 March 1939, FO800/324
c. Lindsay correspondence, cited in Olivia James (ed), Elizabeth Sherman Hoyt Lindsay, *Letters, 1911–1954* (New York, 1960), p. 236; 18 May 1939, British Embassy, Washington, DC, archives.
d. Hope Ridings Miller, *Embassy Row* (New York: Holt, Rinehart and Winston, 1969), p. 195.
e. *Washington Post*, 9 June 1939.
Churchill at the Embassy (pp. 70–71)
a. 'Christmas at the Embassy – December 1941', 14 January 1942, British Embassy, Washington, DC, archives. Used with the kind permission of David Giles.
Halifax (page 73)
a. John Colville, *The Fringes of Power: Downing Street Diaries 1939–55* (London: Hodder and Stoughton, 1985), 20 December 1940, p. 321.
b. Cited in Roy Jenkins, *Churchill* (London: Macmillan, 2001), p. 174.
c. Cited in Nicholas Cull, 'Lord Halifax, 1941–46', in Michael F. Hopkins et al (eds), *The Washington Embassy: British Ambassadors to the United States, 1937–77* (Basingstoke: Palgrave, Macmillan, 2009), p. 36.
d. Cited in Jenkins, *Churchill*, p. 174.
e. Halifax to Churchill, 13 March 1941, National Archives, Kew, UK, PREM 4/27/9.
f. Cited in Andrew Roberts, *The Holy Fox: A Biography of Lord Halifax* (London: Weidenfeld & Nicolson, 1997), p. 286.
New Realities: Adjusting to the Post-War World, 1945–56 (notes to pp. 79–87)
1. David Dimbleby and David Reynolds, *An Ocean Apart: The Relationship between Britain and America in the Twentieth Century* (New York: Random House, 1988), p. 180.
2. 'Mr Churchill and the loan', 14 March 1946, National Archives, Kew, UK, FO 800/513.
3. Inverchapel to Bevin, 22 December 1947, FO 800/514.
4. Churchill, Speech at Westminster College, Fulton, Missouri, 5 March 1946, Churchill Papers, CHUR 5/4A.
5. Truman, Message to Congress, 12 March 1947, Doc 171, 80th Congress, 1st session, Records of House of Representatives, Group 223; National Archives.
6. Dean Acheson, *Present at the Creation: My Years at the State Department* (New York: Norton, 1969), p. 323.
7. Paul Nitze cited in Alex Danchev, *Oliver Franks: Founding Father* (Oxford: Clarendon Press, 1993), p. 118.
8. Franks to Attlee, 15 July 1950, National Archives, Kew, PREM 8/1405.
9. Cabinet Minutes, 25 July 1950, National Archives, Kew, CABINET 50 (50).
10. Cited in Danchev, *Oliver Franks*, p. 130.
11. Cited in Dimbleby and Reynolds, *An Ocean Apart*, p. 207.
12. Franks to Eden, 27 January 1952, FO 371/97593.
13. 'Makins, Sir Roger', NARA, College Park, MD, RG 59, Central Decimal Files 1955–59, Box 2304.
14. Makins to Eden, 9 January 1953, Bodleian Library, Oxford, Sherfield Papers, Box 525.
15. Cited in Dimbleby and Reynolds, *An Ocean Apart*, p. 206.
16. Ibid., p. 215.
17. Cited in Robin Renwick, *Fighting with Allies : America and Britain at Peace and in War* (New York: Times Books, 1996), p. 196
18. Makins to Selwyn-Lloyd, 14 August 1956, Bodleian Library, Oxford, Sherfield Papers, Box 528.
19. Saul Kelly, 'Roger Makins, 1953–56', in Michael F. Hopkins et al (eds), *The Washington Embassy: British Ambassadors to the United States, 1937–77* (Basingstoke: Palgrave Macmillan, 2009), p. 104.
20. Lord Sherfield, unpublished memoirs, Bodleian Library, Oxford, Sherfield Papers, Box 957.
21. Cited in Dimbleby and Reynolds, *An Ocean Apart*, p. 230.
Restoring the Relationship: From Ike to JFK, 1956–63 (notes to pp. 88–93)
1. Roger Makins' valedictory dispatch, 30 November 1956, National Archives, Kew, UK, PREM 11/2189.
2. Cited in James Ellison, 'Harold Caccia, 1956–61', in Michael F. Hopkins et al (eds), *The Washington Embassy: British Ambassadors to the United States, 1937–77* (Basingstoke: Palgrave Macmillan, 2009), p. 114.
3. Eisenhower, phone calls, 16 July 1956, Dwight D. Eisenhower Presidential Library, Abilene, KS.
4. Caccia, Sir Harold Anthony, August 1956, NARA, College Park, MD, RG 59, Central Decimal Files 1955–59, Box 2304.
5. Caccia to Lloyd, 1 January 1957, National Archives, Kew, UK, PREM 11/2189.
6. Peter Catterall (ed.), *The Macmillan Diaries*, vol. 2 (London: Macmillan, 2009), 21 March 1957, p. 23.
7. Cited in Ellison, 'Harold Caccia, 1956–61', p. 121.
8. Arthur Schlesinger, *A Thousand Days: John F. Kennedy in the White House* (Boston, MA: Houghton Mifflin, 1965), p. 375.
9. *The Macmillan Diaries*, vol. 2, entry for 11 June 1961, pp. 389–90.
10. Caccia to Home, 14 July 1961, National Archives, Kew, UK, FCO 371/456139.
11. David Ormsby Gore, Oral History, John F. Kennedy Presidential Library, Boston, MA, JFK #1, 3 December 1965, p. 35.
12. Macmillan to Kennedy, 19 August 1962, Bodleian Library, Oxford, MS Macmillan C 345.
13. Cited in in Robin Renwick, *Fighting with Allies: America and Britain at Peace and in War* (New York: Times Books, 1996), p. 258.
14. Ormsby Gore to Home, 4 December1961, National Archives, Kew, UK, PREM 11/4166.
15. Cited in 'The British government's view of the Cuban missile crisis', *Contemporary Record*, vol. 10, no. 3, p. 34.
16. Cited in David Dimbleby and David Reynolds, *An Ocean Apart: The Relationship between Britain and America in the Twentieth Century* (New York: Random House, 1988), p. 257.
17. Cited in Hopkins, 'David Ormsby Gore, Lord Harlech, 1961–65', p. 139.
18. Macmillan to Kennedy, 21 December 1962, Kennedy Presidential Library, Box 127.
19. Interview with Lord Wright of Richmond, 5 July 2013.
Jack and David (page 90)
a. Alistair Horne, *Macmillan 1957–1986* (London: Macmillan, 1989), p. 307.
b. Interview with Christopher Everett, 19 July 2013.
c. Ormsby Gore to Home, 19 September 1962, National Archives, PREM 11/4166.
d. Michael Hopkins, 'David Ormsby Gore, Lord Harlech, 1961–65', in Hopkins et al, *The Washington Embassy*, p. 135.
The New Chancery (page 93)
a. Cited in Mark Bertram, *Room for Diplomacy: Britain's Diplomatic Buildings Overseas, 1800–2000* (Reading: Spire Books, c2011), p. 316.
A Difficult Period: LBJ and Wilson, Nixon and Heath, 1963–76 (notes to pp. 94–7)
1. Interview with Christopher Everett, 19 July 2013.
2. LBJ tapes, 15 January 1964, #1362, available at http://millercenter.org/scripps/archive/presidentialrecordings/johnson/1964/01 1964.
3. George Ball, cited in David Dimbleby and David Reynolds, *An Ocean Apart: The Relationship between Britain and America in the Twentieth Century* (New York: Random House, 1988), p. 264.
4. Bundy to Johnson, 10 December 1964, *Foreign Relations of the United States (FRUS)*, vol. XIII, p. 158.
5. Cited in Jonathan Colman, 'Patrick Dean, 1965–69', in Michael F. Hopkins et al (eds), *The Washington Embassy: British Ambassadors to the United States, 1937–77* (Basingstoke: Palgrave Macmillan, 2009), p. 153.
6. Dean to Henderson, 15 May 1965, National Archives, Kew, UK, FCO 73/4.
7. Oral History of Sir John Killick, Churchill College, Cambridge, British Diplomatic Oral History Project (BDOHP), p. 15.
8. This cited in Robin Renwick, *Fighting with Allies: America and Britain at Peace and in War* (New York: Times Books, 1996), p. 280.
9. Cited in Colman, 'Patrick Dean, 1965–69, p. 162.
10. Kathleen Burk, *Old World, New World* (London, Little Brown, 2007), p. 620.
11. Cited in Renwick, *Fighting with Allies*, p. 290.
12. Interview with Henry Kissinger, 18 January 2013.
13. Cited in Renwick, *Fighting with Allies*, p. 291.
14. Freeman to Greenhill, 5 June 1970, National Archives, Kew, UK, FCO 73/131.
15. Mr Freeman's Farewell Despatch, 8 January 1971, FCO 82/42.
16. Oral History of Lord Powell, Churchill College, Cambridge, BDOHP.
17. Cited in Alexander Spelling, 'Lord Cromer, 1971–74', in Hopkins et al, *The Washington Embassy*, p. 192.
18. 'Note for the Record': Freeman's meeting with the Prime Minister, 23 July 1970, National Archives, Kew, PREM 15/609.
19. Cited in Renwick, *Fighting with Allies*, p. 298.
20. 'Annual Assessment for the United Kingdom', 14 February 1972, NARA, Pol 1 UK–US.
21. Nixon tapes, 3 February 1973, Richard M. Nixon Presidential Library, Yorba Linda, CA, # 840-12.
22. Cited in Burk, *Old World, New World*, p. 621.
23. Nixon comment from Nixon Tapes, 27 February 1973, Nixon Presidential Library, #486-7(B); Interview with Henry Kissinger, 18 January 2013.
24. Cited in Spelling, 'Lord Cromer, 1971–74', p. 202.
The Beatles at the Embassy (page 96)
a. This section (including all quotes) based on Bob Spitz, *The Beatles* (New York: Little Brown, 2005), pp. 477–8.
Special Relationships: Towards the Thatcher Decade, 1976–90 (notes to pp. 98–103)
1. Palliser to Owen, 28 April 1977, National Archives, Kew, UK, FCO 73/290.
2. Cited in R. Roy, 'Peter Ramsbotham, 1974–77', in Michael F. Hopkins et al (eds), *The Washington Embassy: British Ambassadors to the United States, 1937–77* (Basingstoke: Palgrave Macmillan, 2009), p. 224.
3. Zbigniew Brzezinski, *Power and Principle: Memoirs of the National Security Adviser, 1977–1981* (New York: Farrar Straus Giroux, 1985), p. 291.
4. Jay to Callaghan, 22 February 1978. Churchill College, Cambridge, PJAY 02 028.
5. CIA report, 22 October 1979, Jimmy Carter Presidential Library, Atlanta, GA, RAC NLC-7-16-10-14-1.
6. Brzezinski to Carter, 12 May 1979, Carter Presidential Library, Brzezinski Papers.
7. Speech at White House Arrival Ceremony, 17 December 1979, Thatcher Foundation Website.
8. Charles Moore, *Margaret Thatcher: The Authorized Biography*, Vol. 1: *Not for Turning* (London: Allen Lane, 2013), p. 540.
9. Allen to Reagan, 'Your meeting with Prime Minister Thatcher', Ronald Reagan Presidential Library, Simi Valley, CA, Charles Tyson files, Box 4.
10. Henderson, *Mandarin*, 7 February 1981, p. 383.
11. Ronald Reagan, *The Reagan Diaries* (New York: HarperCollins, 2007), 27 February 1981, p. 5
12. Thatcher to Reagan, 5 March 1981, Thatcher Archives, Churchill College, Cambridge, THCR 3/1/13.
13. Interview with Peter Jay, 14 February 2013.
14. Interview with Lord Powell of Bayswater, 13 February 2013.
15. Interview with Lord Renwick of Clifton, 3 June 2013
16. Cited in Moore, *Not for Turning*, p. 636.
17. Ibid., p. 686.
18. Interview with Lord Renwick of Clifton, 3 June 2013.
19. Wright to Pym, 30 September 1982, private collection.
20. George Shultz, *Triumph and Turmoil: My Years as Secretary of State* (New York: Scribner, 1993), p. 152.
21. Memcon, Thatcher and Reagan, 26 October 1983, NARA, Reagan Library, Exec Sec NSC: UK (vol. IV).
22. TV Interview for BBC, 17 December 1984, Thatcher Foundation Website.
23. Thatcher interview, 8 January 1990, Thatcher Foundation Website http://www.margaretthatcher.org/document/109324, last accessed 16 October 2013.
24. Interview with Sir Antony Acland, 21 June 2013.
25. Correspondence with Barbara Bush, 9 August 2013.
26. Interview with Sir Antony Acland, 21 June 2013.
27. Correspondence with Barbara Bush, 9 August 2013.
28. Bush in George Bush and Brent Scowcroft, *A World Transformed* (New York: Knopf, 1998), p. 69.
29. Condoleezza Rice, *Extraordinary, Ordinary People: A Memoir of Family* (New York: Crown Archetype, 2010), p. 261.
'Nicko' Henderson (page 99)
a. Philip Ziegler, *Edward Heath: The Authorised Biography* (London: Harper Press, 2010), p. 529.
b. Interview with Charles Anson, 20 July 2013.
c. Correspondence with Barbara Bush, 9 August 2013.
d. Interview with Charles Anson, 20 July 2013.
e. Nicholas Henderson, *Mandarin: Diaries* (London: Weidenfeld and Nicolson, 1995), diary entry for 26 April 1980, p. 336.
More Recent Times (notes to pp. 104–5)
1. George W. Bush, Address before a Joint Session of Congress, 20 September 2001, Public Papers of the Presidents, Government Printing Office.
■ Part IV (notes to pp. 109–64)
1. Gavin Stamp, 'Lutyens' Washington embassy', in *The British Ambassador's Residence, Washington D.C.: Works of Art from the Government Art Collection* (London: Government Art Collection, 2004).
2. David Barbie, 'Britain adorns our capital city' *Washington Post*, 22 December 1929.
3. Christopher Hussey, 'The British Embassy, Washington DC', *Country Life*, 14 January 1939, p. 41.
4. Peter Wilson, 'New British Embassy graces our capital', *New York Times*, 19 October 1930.
5. Quoted in Gavin Stamp, 'The British Embassy Washington DC, USA', *Country Life*, 30 November 2006, vol. 200, no. 48. Memos, 7 January 1929 and 11 January 1929, quoted in *Lutyens Abroad: The Work of Sir Edward Lutyens Outside the British Isles*, ed. Andrew Hopkins and Gavin Stamp (London: British School at Rome at the British Academy, 2002), p. 140.
6. Interview, Allan Greenberg, 30 July 2013.
7. A. S. G. Butler, *The Architecture of Sir Edwin Lutyens*, 3 vols (London: Country Life, 1950), vol. 2, p. 47.
8. Elizabeth Wilhide, quoted in *Lutyens Abroad*, p. 146.
■ Part V (notes to pp. 169–226)
1. Elizabeth Wilhide, *Sir Edwin Lutyens: Designing in the English Tradition* (London: National Trust Books, 2012), p. 104.
2. Lindsay to Earle, 2 October 1930, National Archives, Kew, UK, FO 10/414; Mark Bertram, *Room for Diplomacy: Britain's Diplomatic Buildings Overseas, 1800–2000* (Reading: Spire Books, 2011), p. 207.
3. Bertram, *Room for Diplomacy*, p. 207.
4. Lady Lindsay to Belmont, 3 November 1932, Olivia James (ed.), Elizabeth Sherman Hoyt Lindsay, *Letters, 1911–1954* (New York, 1960), p. 190.
5. *Washington Post*, 23 April 1935.
6. Lady Lindsay to Belmont, 6 November 1933, James (ed.), *Letters*, p. 203.
7. *Washington Star*, 4 June 1935.

British Ministers/ Ambassadors to the United States

Political Appointee*

Select Bibliography

THE RESIDENCE AND EDWIN LUTYENS

Further reading

BERTRAM, Mark, *Room for Diplomacy: Britain's Diplomatic Buildings Overseas 1800-2000* (Reading: Spire Books, 2011).

BROWN, Jane, *Gardens of a Golden Afternoon: Story of a Partnership: Edwin Lutyens and Gertrude Jekyll* (London: Allen Lane, 1982).

BUTLER, A. S. G., *The Architecture of Sir Edwin Lutyens*, vol. 2 (London: Country Life, 1950).

GREENBERG, Allan, *Lutyens and the Modern Movement* (Winterbourne: Papadakis, 2007).

HOPKINS, Andrew and GREENBERG, Allan, (eds), *Lutyens Abroad: The Work of Sir Edward Lutyens Outside the British Isles* (London: British School at Rome at the British Academy, 2002).

HUSSEY, Christopher, *The Life of Sir Edwin Lutyens* (Woodbridge: Antique Collector's Club, 1984).

LUTYENS, Mary, *Edwin Lutyens* (London: John Murray, 1980).

PERCY, C. and RIDLEY J. (eds), *The Letters of Edwin Lutyens to his wife Lady Emily* (London: Collins, 1985).

RIDLEY, Jane, *Edwin Lutyens: His Life, His Wife, His Work* (London: Pimlico, 2003)

STAMP, Gavin, *Edwin Lutyens Country Houses: From the Archives of Country Life* (London: Aurum Press, 2012).

WILHIDE, Elizabeth, *Sir Edwin Lutyens: Designing in the English Tradition* (London: National Trust Books, 2012).

Archival repositories for primary sources

The National Archives, Kew

The British Architectural Library at the Royal Institute of British Architects (RIBA) (especially Lutyens' handwritten letters, held at the V&A Museum location)

The Archives of the British Embassy, Washington, DC (Embassy Archives)

The Washington Historical Society, Washington, DC

The Library of Congress, Washington, DC

DIPLOMACY AND ANGLO-AMERICAN RELATIONS

General reading

BRANDON, Henry, *Special Relationship: A Foreign Correspondent's Memoirs from Roosevelt to Reagan* (London: Macmillan, 1988).

BURK, Kathleen, *Old World, New World: The Story of Britain and America* (New York: Little Brown, 2007).

DICKIE, John, *"Special" No More. Anglo-American Relations: Rhetoric and Reality* (London: Weidenfeld & Nicholson, 1994).

DIMBLEBY, David and REYNOLDS, David, *An Ocean Apart: The Relationship between Britain and America in the Twentieth Century* (New York: Random House, 1988).

DUMBRELL, John, *A Special Relationship: Anglo-American Relations in the Cold War and After* (London: Macmillan, 2001).

ELLIS, Sylvia, *Historical Dictionary of Anglo-American Relations* (Lanham, MD: Scarecrow Press, 2009).

RENWICK, Robin, *Fighting with Allies: America and Britain in Peace and War* (New York: Times Books; Basingstoke: Macmillan, 1996).

TEMPERLEY, Howard, *Britain and America since Independence* (Basingstoke: Palgrave Macmillan, 2002).

Ambassador-specific works

HOPKINS, M, Kelly S. & YOUNG, J., *The Washington Embassy: British Ambassadors to the United States, 1939-77* (Basingstoke: Palgrave, 2009).

BIRKENHEAD, F. W. F. S., *Halifax: The Life of Lord Halifax* (London: Hamish Hamilton, 1965).

DANCHEV, Alex, *Oliver Franks: Founding Father* (Oxford: Clarendon Press, 1993).

GILLIES, Donald, *Radical Diplomat: The Life of Sir Archibald Clark Kerr, Lord Inverchapel, 1882-1951* (London: I. B. Tauris, 1998).

HENDERSON, Nicholas, *Mandarin: The Diaries of an Ambassador, 1969-1982* (London: Weidenfeld and Nicholson, 1982).

HOPKINS, Michael, *Oliver Franks and the Truman Administration: Anglo-American Relations, 1948-52* (London: Routledge, 2003).

MCKERCHER, B. J. C., *Esme Howard: A Diplomatic Biography* (Cambridge: Cambridge University Press, 1989).

REYNOLDS, David, *Lord Lothian and Anglo-American Relations, 1939-40* (Philadelphia: American Philosophical Society, 1983)

ROBERTS, Andrew, *"The Holy Fox": A Life of Lord Halifax* (London: Weidenfeld and Nicholson, 1991).

Archival repositories for primary sources

The National Archives, Kew

National Archives, Carlisle (for Esme Howard's papers)

Churchill College, Cambridge (for the Churchill and Thatcher papers; also a collection of Lord Halifax's papers and those of Peter Jay)

Bodleian Library, Oxford University (for the papers of Roger Makins (Lord Sherfield) and Harold Macmillan)

The National Archives and Records Administration, College Park, MD

The Presidential Libraries of the United States

The Library of Congress

THE ORCHID COLLECTION

General reading

RITTERSHAUSEN, Wilma and RITTERSHAUSEN, Brian, *The Amazing World of Orchids* (London: Quadrille, for The Royal Horticultural Society, 2010).

Index

Photographic Credits

t: top, b: bottom, l: left, r: right

Acknowledgements

Our chief debt is to the present ambassador, Sir Peter Westmacott, and his wife Susan Nemazee Westmacott who has driven the project from day one with formidable energy and imagination. We have also been most fortunate to have a publisher with the skill and patience of Suzanne Tise-Isoré, who is *sans pareil* in the world of illustrated books. At Flammarion, Sarah Rozelle and Bernard Lagacé have been outstanding throughout. We are also grateful to our marvellous photographers, Eric Sander (the house and garden) and James Osen (the orchids).

We owe much to the Residence staff, particularly Amanda Downes, the Social Secretary, whose knowledge of the Embassy is greater than any living figure. We would also like to thank John Sonnier, Pierre Gilissen, Yatman Gurung, Fay Gibson and Laurence Dennis and his team.

Penny Johnson and Julia Toffolo at the Government Art Collection are masters of their craft, as their impressive contributions demonstrate. We would also like to thank Allan Greenberg, Kenneth Doggett, Candia Peterson and Martin Lutyens (for expertise on Lutyens and architecture); Joseph Francis, and Julian Shaw at the RHS (for all things orchid) and Nobuko Sasae and Kiyomi Buker (for research in Japan).

Many academics and writers have helped us directly or indirectly. They include Mark Bertram, Michael Beschloss, Kathleen Burk, Jane Ridley, Adam Smith, Judith Tankard and David Reynolds. Michael Hopkins, Saul Kelly and John Young deserve special thanks for their invaluable edited volume on the Embassy. We are also grateful to so many talented research archivists, on both sides of the Atlantic, too numerous to mention by name.

Our sincere thanks to all our kind interviewees, including Sir Antony Acland, Charles Anson, Barbara Bush, Christopher Everett, Peter Jay, Henry Kissinger, Sir David and Lady Manning, Sir Christopher and Lady Meyer, Jonathan Powell, Lord Powell of Bayswater, David Reynolds, Lord Renwick of Clifton, Sir Nigel Sheinwald, Adam Smith and Lord Wright of Richmond.

At Wellington College, Anthony would like to thank Angela Reed and Paula Maynard, student Peter Openshaw, art historians Edward Twohig and Adam Rattray, Jonathan Meakin for research help, and his wife Joanna for constant support. Daniel would like to thank Charles Moore for his forbearance, Laurence Norman for intellectual inspiration, and his wife Sonja for making everything seem possible.

© Flammarion, SA, Paris, 2014

All rights reserved. No part of this
publication may be reproduced
in any form or by any means, electronic,
photocopy, information retrieval
system or otherwise, without written
permission from Flammarion SA.

Flammarion SA
87, quai Panhard et Levassor
75647 Paris Cedex 13
France

editions.flammarion.com
styleetdesign-flammarion.com

Dépôt légal: 05/2014
14 15 16 3 2 1
ISBN: 978-2-08-129902-3

EXECUTIVE EDITOR
Suzanne Tise-Isoré
Style & Design Collection

PROJECT EDITOR, BRITISH EMBASSY
Susan Nemazee Westmacott

EDITORIAL MANAGEMENT
Sarah Rozelle

EDITORIAL ASSISTANCE
Lucie Lurton

GRAPHIC DESIGN
Bernard Lagacé

COPYEDITING
Sarah Newton

PROOFREADING
Helen Downey

INDEXING
Joan Dearnley

PRODUCTION
Élodie Conjat-Cuvelier

COLOUR SEPARATION
Les Artisans du Regard, Paris

PRINTED BY
Toppan Leefung, China

CAMPBELL
LUTYENS
LONDON · NEW YORK · HONG KONG

This book was published with the help
of John Campbell, Chairman and Co-Founder
of Campbell Lutyens and Co. Ltd

RIGHT This bronze statue of Winston Churchill was unveiled in April 1966 and is on permanent loan from the English Speaking Union. Located next to Massachusetts Avenue, Churchill's front foot stands on American soil but his back foot remains on British soil, in the grounds of the Embassy.